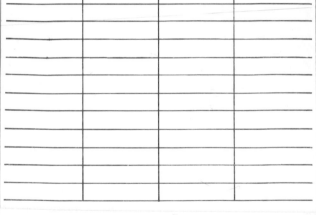

Highlights.
for Children

Growing Up Writing

Lov is
HeLPing
SmBdy RiT.

Highlights.
for Children

Growing Up Writing

Sharing with Your Children
the Joys of Good Writing

Linda Leonard Lamme, Ph.D.

Foreword by Walter B. Barbe, Ph.D., Editor-in-Chief, *Highlights for Children*

ACROPOLIS BOOKS LTD.
WASHINGTON, D.C.

ACROPOLIS BOOKS, Ltd.
Colortone Building, 2400 17th Street, N.W.
Washington, D.C. 20009

Printed in the United States of America by
COLORTONE PRESS
Creative Graphics, Inc.
Washington, D.C. 20009

Attention: Schools and Corporations
ACROPOLIS books are available at quantity discounts with bulk purchase for educational, business, or sales promotional use. For further information, please write to: SPECIAL SALES DEPARTMENT, ACROPOLIS BOOKS, LTD., 2400 17th ST., N.W., WASHINGTON, D.C. 20009.

Are there Acropolis Books you want but cannot find in your local stores?
You can get any Acropolis book title in print. Simply send title and retail price, plus 50 cents for postage and handling costs for each book desired. District of Columbia residents add applicable sales tax. Enclose check or money order only, no cash please, to: ACROPOLIS BOOKS, LTD., 2400 17th ST., N.W., WASHINGTON, D.C. 20009.

Photos by Gene Gissin

Library of Congress Cataloging in Publication Data

Lamme, Linda Leonard.
  Growing Up Writing.

  Written in cooperation with the children's magazine, Highlights for Children.
  Includes index.
  1. English language—Composition and exercises.
2. Penmanship. 3. Spelling. 4. Domestic education.
I. Highlights for Children, Inc. II. Title
LB1576.L26   1984   649'.68   84-14512
ISBN 0-87491-758-1
ISBN 0-87491-760-3 (pbk.)

Dedication

**For my husband, Ary,
and my daughter, Laurel Agnes**

Acknowledgements

I appreciate the fact that my family has been tremendously
supportive of this writing endeavor. I am grateful to doctoral
students Beulah Ayris, Nancye Childers, Beth Clark, Connie Green,
Sharen Halsall, Sandra Kolb, and Sharon Rosenthal for their
enthusiasm about children's writing and for their research studies
from which I learned a great deal.

The staff of *Highlights* and Debbie Salem have been most helpful in
editing the manuscript.

Contents

Foreword

My work with *Highlights for Children* often takes me into schools and parent organizations where I've observed the importance of children's writing. As an editor and teacher, I know that there is an extremely high correlation between reading and writing, and that a person who cannot write, cannot think.

There is no doubt that parents are eager to help their children develop this most essential skill. They realize that schools simply cannot accomplish this task alone. Moreover, studies show that writing experiences at home far outweigh school experiences in contributing to a child's development. The parents' role is critical, but in the past I have found very few guides that we at *Highlights* could recommend to parents.

We are delighted, therefore, to be able to work with Dr. Lamme on *Growing Up Writing*. This respected early childhood educator shares our conviction that children are creative and that the sooner they begin writing, the better. She has carefully integrated these two concepts into her book. It is full of activities for children which demonstrate the kind of "fun with a purpose" that we at *Highlights* believe in so strongly. It is also a practical guide for parents, demonstrating how writing can be introduced into the home, making it an activity the entire family can share and enjoy together.

In *Growing Up Writing*, Dr. Lamme offers fascinating insights into how children learn, enabling you to enjoy this magic process as it unfolds in your child. She suggests easy, practical ways for creating writing and drawing centers in the home, so your child will want to do both. She shows you truly how, as her daughter put it, "Love is helping smbdy rit."

Highlights for Children is proud to be a part of *Growing Up Writing*. We believe it will prove to be an exciting and stimulating book for your family.

Walter B. Barbe, Ph.D.
Editor-in-Chief, *Highlights for Children*

Introduction

The other night, I had to attend a meeting which lasted past my daughter's bedtime. I returned home and was brushing my teeth prior to going to bed when I looked up, and there on the bathroom mirror was a note in the shape of a heart. It said, "Hi, Mom! I Love You. Laurel." I got a pair of scissors, cut a heart out of a piece of paper, and taped a note next to hers, saying, "I Love You, Too, Laurel Love, Mom," which she read in the morning.

Our family has found that by integrating writing into our daily activities, we become more thoughtful of each other. At the same time, our daughter is learning to enjoy writing and becoming a skilled writer.

Illustration 1

My interest in children's writing began when I was an elementary school teacher. I found that some children claimed to hate writing, while others loved it. They frequently wrote with strong emotion and communicated in writing things they would not have mentioned when talking to me. I learned how influential parents can be as children learn to write.

When our daughter first began to scribble, I became fascinated with her work, for I found that scribbling is far more complex and important than I had realized. Her scribbles, aside from being lovely art objects, revealed a lot about her understanding of the world of writing.

Gradually, our family began writing a great deal. I saw that writing helped Laurel learn how to read. By observing my own child and her friends and by reading professional books, I gained many insights into how writing develops and how parents can help children become avid writers.

Research has shown that parents are supportive of their children's reading and drawing, offering praise for their work and commenting positively about their efforts. But when their children write, parents are critical. They point out mistakes and expect children to correct their work. Children's attitudes toward writing are influenced by their parents' responses to writing.

In workshops I conduct for parents, I'm asked many questions:

- How can I make writing more pleasant for my child?
- My child writes many of his letters backwards. What can I do about that?
- When should I teach my child how to write?
- How can I teach my child to form alphabet letters?
- How can I encourage my child to write more neatly?
- How can I help my child write more interesting stories?
- How can I help my child revise his writing?
- How can I help my child proofread?
- Where can my child publish his poem?
- Why doesn't my child's teacher correct her writing papers?
- My child writes so slowly that it takes him half an hour to

write two sentences. How can I help him speed up?

You'll find answers to these and other questions in this book.

It is my hope that as you read this book you will get "hooked on writing." You'll make writing an integral part of your family's experiences and your children will become avid writers. If you have experiences you would like to share, please write to me:

Linda L. Lamme, Ph.D.
Elementary and Early Childhood Education
2215 Norman Hall
University of Florida
Gainesville, FL 32611

Chapter 1

Writing Today

"**B**ut I don't need to learn how to write. I'll have a secretary when I grow up."
"Why write, when you can give him a call?"
"Wow, now I like what that says."

Parents are reacting with varying degrees of frustration and concern to the quality of education being offered their children in the public schools. And because of the general decline in writing skills, more emphasis is being given to writing instruction in schools.

There are both educational and social reasons for the decline in writing ability. Writing at home is less common than it was in the days before the telephone. Today, fewer family members keep journals or diaries than in the days before television. Writing is less central to school instruction than it was in the days before textbooks and workbooks, when children wrote out problems and took notes in notebooks. Today's children have more discussion in school and write only to fill in the blanks. Jobs today require less writing and more talking (or telephoning) than they previously did. Photojournalism and telecommunications are replacing journalistic writing in newspapers, newsmagazines, and other print media.

At home, in school, on the job, and in society in general, writing and, to a lesser extent, reading have taken a back seat to the communication skills of listening and speaking.

This is a problem for society. Industrial sources claim that they lose hundreds of dollars due to the poor handwriting skills of their employees. This loss is compounded by the lack of precise written language for training materials, repair manuals, and instruction booklets. Poor writing costs industry millions of dollars annually.

The Benefits of Writing

As a parent, you probably realize the importance of reading to children. Reading campaigns encourage you to read aloud to your child. It is common knowledge that children who enter school with five years of assistance in learning to read have a far easier time in school than children who have not been read to. Do you recognize, however, the importance of writing? Children who write well are inevitably good readers, but the reverse is not necessarily true. Why is learning to write well so important?

Writing not only helps your child learn to write, but also assists in his or her efforts at learning to read. As you write for your young children, it is easy for them to observe how alphabet letters form words, how words move from left to right, and most important, how written materials have meaning. When older children write, they think about sequence, cause and effect, and other reading comprehension skills.

In addition to assisting with the reading process, writing helps your child think in a way that talking or reading cannot. Before a person talks, he or she seldom consciously outlines the details of what he or she wants to say. But before a person writes, he or she needs to plan and structure the communication. The writer must think about what to say and how to say it.

Writing can help your child communicate. The written word is often far more powerful than the spoken word, especially for children. Writing almost always receives a response. Children gain positive adult attention by writing little secret messages, notes, or requests. Older children receive accolades for the stories and books that they write.

Writing helps develop self-concept. There is a tremendous sense of power attached to making meaningful marks on paper. The gleam in your child's eye when he has first learned to write his name or has seen his first story published is unforgettable.

Writing may help your child learn to become sensitive to the views of others. When writing to someone else, he may think about his audience's views. You have to be able to see another's point of view to communicate effectively.

Writing can help young children understand that print has meaning. Your child notices signs, labels, and other print in the environment. Before children write, rarely is such attention given to the print which permeates the environment.

Writing may be an escape for emotions. If your child is too shy to demonstrate affection verbally he might write, "I love you." If your child is angry he might scribble "I hate you," on scrap paper to vent frustrations, rid himself of anger, and get on with other things.

Writing may help your child learn to make decisions. All composing is a series of decision-making processes. What should I write about? How should I say it? Who will read it? Which word will communicate most effectively? Is that word spelled correctly? These are only a few of the many questions that pass through a writer's mind during the composing process.

Writing may help your child develop a longer attention span. Schools complain because children are not able to sit down and "work." Children today spend too much time in passive activities such as watching television. Learning to write requires active participation on the part of children. They become engrossed in drawing and writing and often stay at a task for long periods of time, building up endurance for paper and pencil activities of their own creation.

Most important, both you and your child will enjoy writing. Parents are often the recipients of numerous "I love you" notes and other beautifully written pieces. As you watch your child's writing develop, you'll be amazed by the progress he is making. You will enjoy some precious moments of parent-child interaction.

When to Begin

At what age can you begin assisting your child in becoming a writer? You can begin by reading to your child at birth. All the reading you do during the first years aids writing development by exposing your child to writing. Just before one year of age, your baby can be given (under supervision) his first writing tools—water-soluble markers and large sheets of paper. His writing experiences will have begun.

Since progress in writing is dependent upon children's experiences with writing tools, chronological ages are not discussed in this book. What one child does at age two, another may not do until age five or six if the latter has had little exposure to markers, chalk, crayons, or pencils. Some children never pick up a pencil until the day they enter school. They pass through the "stages" discussed in this book much more rapidly than younger children. But, in order to have the necessary foundation for writing, they need to be given the opportunity to progress just as younger children do, from scribbling to writing.

Fundamental Assumptions about Writing at Home

This book provides a multitude of ideas for children's writing as well as a strong rationale for writing in your home. These are based upon the following premises:

• You are your child's first and most important teacher. Your attitudes toward writing and the writing that goes on in your home informally "teach" your child a lot about writing.

• You don't need to buy workbooks or formal instructional materials in order to help your child become a good writer. There are many natural opportunities for writing in your daily routines that are more fun for children and more effective than school materials.

• You need to provide time, space, and materials for writing. Other family diversions such as watching television usurp time which might better be spent talking, going places, reading, and writing.

• You need to monitor what goes on in your child's school so that you can supplement and support that instruction at home.

• In many ways, writing resembles other skills, such as reading, running, playing a musical instrument, and participating in athletic events; the more you practice, the better you become, and the more proficient you become, the more you enjoy writing.

Chapter 2

The Writing Environment

"Hey, Dad, buy me some new markers, please?"
"Where's the tape? I can't find it anywhere!"
"But I left you a note!"

Your home environment has a powerful impact on your child's behavior and development. If your child grows up in a home rich with books, magazines, and newspapers, he values reading and is likely to acquire early reading skills. Similarly, if your home provides space, materials, and opportunities for writing, he learns the importance of writing. An environment which involves young children with the written word and provides many opportunities for drawing and writing goes a long way toward nurturing a writer. Older children, too, need space, materials, and opportunities for writing if they are to develop lifelong writing habits and become accomplished writers.

Vertical Places for Writing and Drawing

If you have a small child, he will enjoy writing and drawing in two types of places: "stand-up places" and "sit-down places." Stand-up places are essential for toddlers who enjoy "writing on the run" and helpful for older children in communicating briefly with each other and their parents. There are a number of ways to provide these kinds of writing and drawing opportunities.

Chalkboards
Find or make a chalkboard—the larger the better for very young

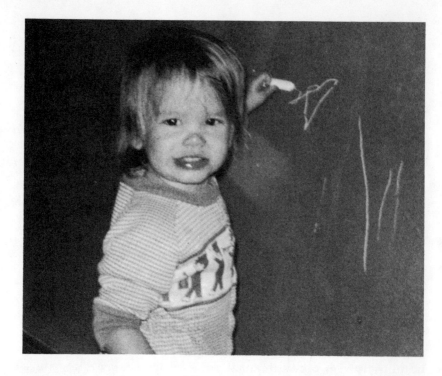

Illustration 2

children. You can make one by painting a large, very sturdy piece of cardboard with chalkboard paint. Since your youngster is standing up and using pressure to write and draw, make the board very sturdy. One that bounces will be hard to write on and may frustrate children.

Put the chalkboard in a central location where it will get lots of use. A hallway or a child's room is a good place. Buy thick, soft chalk because regular-size chalk breaks easily. Although it's messier, soft chalk makes dark marks more easily than hard chalk.

Another way to give your child experience with drawing is to let him "paint" with water on a wall or chalkboard. Take the chalkboard outside for this activity. Use brushes that are light enough for your child to handle easily.

Murals

Murals are another "stand-up" writing and drawing experience. You can tape large sheets of newsprint, available from most newspaper offices, computer paper, shelf paper, butcher paper, or brown wrapping paper to a sturdy, flat surface (refrigerator door, wall, chalkboard, or door). Thick markers or thick tempera paints are best for painting on a mural or easel. Paint drips from vertical surfaces, so if a large, flat floor or table space is available, that is preferable. Murals are particularly enjoyable activities for several children to do together. They make great play-group activities.

You might label pictures of foods, animals, or transportation vehicles made into a collage. Murals make good backdrops for puppet plays. Children's murals make attractive decorations for otherwise bare walls in hallways, utility rooms, or children's rooms.

Memo Boards
If you have a child who is beginning to write or who can already write, a small chalkboard or memo board is ideal for sending messages from one family member to another. One family mounted a memo board on a bathroom wall. Daily, the parents and babysitters wrote and received messages from their child. At first she wrote "I love you" messages. As time went on, her messages became more elaborate. Her babysitters asked her questions such as, "Do you want to go for a walk around the block?" to which she could respond with a simple, "yes" or "no." Her dad asked, "Would you like to go to the ice cream shop for a treat after supper?" At first, she responded, "Yes!" When the question appeared a few weeks later, she copied much of his question in her response, "Yes, I'd like to go to the ice cream shop." And, when the same question appeared several weeks later, her response was original: "Yes, I want chokit!"

Another family has a memo board by the phone. In addition to recording phone messages, one month they decided that each day each family member had to write something nice on the board. That board became the center of a lot of good feeling on the part of family members.

What You Can Do to Help
You can write on the chalkboard long before your child can read. In fact, such writing aids the development of reading. Parents in

one family wrote "secret messages" to their daughter each day. They were "secret" because the child could not yet read. "Let's bake a cake today;" "Uncle Ed comes to visit today;" or "What shall we give Grandma for Christmas?" were some examples. The parents pointed to each word as they read it to the child, who was so interested that she memorized the message. Whenever visitors came to the house or babysitters arrived, the child would bring them to her room to "read" her secret message to them.

These same parents discovered that when they wrote the words to a familiar song on the chalkboard, their child could recognize the song! After that, songs became secret messages for a while.

You might play games at the chalkboard, writing short, repetitive sentences:

> Tanya is a girl.
> David is a boy.
> Tosh is a cat.
> Tarki is a dog.
> Audrey is a doll.

Your child will memorize the sentences and read them to anyone who'll listen. He may also color in some of the words and alphabet letters, playing with the writing. He might try to copy your writing. So the chalkboard can be an excellent medium for introducing your child to reading and writing.

Memo boards need your interaction to be effective. They can be the focus of family communication and entertainment. In addition to sending messages, family members can share jokes and riddles on a memo board.

A Writing and Drawing Center

No matter how old your child is, he needs a personal space for writing. Beginning at age one, you need a child-size table (the larger the writing surface the better) and chairs.

Although the table should be low in height, if the writing surface is too small, the table will become cluttered and your child will resort to making tiny pictures and notes or will avoid writing altogether. A large surface, on the other hand, allows

Illustration 3

for twelve-by-eighteen-inch pieces of paper, which encourage longer and more complex writing.

Illustration 3 shows a writing center for a child. Try to find a child-size table with a smooth top when you are furnishing a child's writing center in your home. It is easier for a child to write when his feet are touching the floor rather than dangling in the air, so a child-size table is best. Try to place the table in a well-lit area. Let your child mark on the table if he wishes to, since even the most meticulous writer ventures beyond the edge of the paper once in a while! If there is room, include a place for you or another adult to offer assistance when your child requests it. This extra space will also make it more comfortable for several children to write and draw together.

An older child needs a desk of his own which offers privacy and storage space. He'll need ready access to a variety of enticing materials such as paper, writing tools, and other accessories. Sometimes, even with his own special place to write and draw, your child will prefer to write with you nearby. The sociability of writing together overcomes any disadvantages like not having feet on the floor. So, in addition to providing a special place for writing, you may want to invite your child to write with you: "I'm writing a letter to Granny. Want to write a note to send with it?"

Writing Can Happen Everywhere

In addition to writing at stand-up and sit-down places especially set aside for writing, children who are avid writers will write in many other places around the house. Your child might enjoy stretching out on the floor to draw, paint, or write. The floor is especially appropriate for painting activities for which a large, flat surface is needed. Writing on the floor does not encourage the development of good handwriting skills, but if your child is writing at tables as well, he can focus on handwriting when he is seated and use the floor for more casual writing.

Your child might like to write when he travels. Again, his handwriting will not be its best, but traveling is more fun when you write travelogues, diaries, postcards, and letters.

Your child will also enjoy writing where you write. If you type, your child will want a turn at the typewriter or word processor. If you have a small portable table or T.V. tray that could be used for writing and drawing, let him move it next to you. The kitchen table provides a good writing surface when you are cooking.

Supplies

If you provide a variety of materials, you will increase the likelihood that your child will become an avid writer. The basic supplies of paper, writing tools, and accessories always stimulate writing. You'll need to buy some of these but others are free, if you know where to look!

Paper

Your child will enjoy using all kinds of paper. The size, shape, and texture of paper influence what children draw or write. For example, if you provide folded paper, your child is more likely to make a greeting card; if you provide stationery, personal letters will result. Tiny scraps will emerge as little personal notes or labels, while large sheets will become mural-like landscapes.

There are many types of papers that you might include as basic supplies for your child's writing center.

Note pads, especially small ones with colored pages cut into interesting shapes, are fun. Your child can tear out pages and give them to friends. He can draw or write a sequence of pictures or messages on one page after another. You can take pocket-size pads on trips.

Construction paper is a standby for most families, and there are different grades available. Some are of medium weight and tear rather easily; heavyweight paper is better. Some construction papers are produced in rather bland colors; others are more vibrant. The mixed (or rainbow-colored) construction paper sets will give your child variety, but he will prefer the light colors, so they will get used up more quickly than the dark colors. Chalk or light crayon colors are practically the only way to draw on dark paper, but dark scraps can be used for collage work and for pasting upon lighter colors. In addition to a rainbow set, you'll need solid color sets of red (Valentine's Day and Christmas), orange (Halloween and Thanksgiving), green (Christmas and St. Patrick's Day), white, and yellow. Besides having a stack of construction paper handy, you'll want to provide a scrap box for various sizes and shapes of paper that are left over. If you staple together several pieces of construction paper, your child will be able to write stories and illustrate them in book form.

Newsprint is another basic paper supply. Since markers bleed through newsprint, crayons work best on this paper. Newsprint is inexpensive, and in many cases, free from printing or newspaper offices. It can be used as scrap paper or stretched out for a mural. Your child might like to decorate newsprint to use as wrapping paper. Butcher paper can be used in similar ways.

Stationery is prized by most children. Stationery kits and paper that is printed with your child's name on it are sure to generate some correspondence. Current, Inc. (Colorado Springs, CO 80941) offers children's stationery kits. Sometimes children enjoy writing paper that they themselves have made. You can transform plain white paper into stationery by affixing stickers to it or by drawing or writing on it. Another interesting way to make writing paper is to cut pictures out of old catalogues and to paste them onto paper. Pictures of toys or pieces of used wrapping paper make especially good designs for children's note paper. For example, two girls got together, cut up catalogues containing jewelry and Christmas items, made stationery and then sold it at a bazaar prior to Christmas.

Illustration 4

Some easy printing techniques include styrofoam prints and vegetable prints. You can draw a pattern into styrofoam with a ball-point pen. Potato prints are made by carving designs in potatoes. Your child can draw an outline onto a sponge and cut it out to make prints. Carving and cutting should always be done under careful supervision.

Postcards provide another form of stationery for short messages that young children can write easily.

Scraps are the best types of paper to have available. Practically every business establishment has scrap paper. Printing companies either distribute scrap paper free or else sell it for a nominal charge. Businesses and universities discard computer-printout paper. The light green lines on this paper make writing easy if your child is used to lined paper in school. The sources of scrap paper are endless. Scrap paper is sometimes stronger than construction paper and often more colorful, too.

Lined paper, similar to school paper, makes it easy for your child to write. Usually, teachers can either send home paper with appropriately spaced lines or recommend places where it can be purchased. Regular notebook paper is fine. If your child can't write small enough to fit the lines, he'll automatically use double spaces.

Blank books make wonderful homes for the stories in your child's head. Wallpaper scraps make excellent covers for such books. Your child will more likely value and keep his writings in this more permanent format.

The essential element in paper supply is variety. You'll go through several pieces of paper a day if your child is an avid writer or artist. You need both quantity and variety of paper to supply his needs.

Writing and Drawing Tools

Besides paper, your child needs a variety of tools with which to write and draw. Large, fat tools are more suitable for drawing on large paper, while small, thin tools generate writing or sketching on smaller pieces of paper. Very young children need different tools for scribbling than those used by children who are just learning to write, and beginning writers, in turn, need different tools than accomplished writers.

If your child is very young, the best drawing tools are water-soluble markers. Markers color brightly with little pressure. Their tips are blunt, making them ideal for scribbling, no matter what part of the tip reaches the paper. Although the colors wash out of most fabrics, it is advisable for very young children to wear smocks while painting or drawing. One of your old t-shirts is a perfect coverup. When your child puts on smocks before painting or coloring, he feels as though he is about to participate in a special event.

Shortly after exposure to thick, water-soluble markers, your child begins to refine his scribbles. At this point, thin (regular pen-size) markers with a medium width of stroke are

Illustration 5

best. Given a choice, children almost always select markers over pencils or crayons for writing. Markers make clear lines with little pressure. They are colorful and young children love to experiment with color. Remember that mistakes don't bother children nearly as much as they bother adults. Children would rather scratch out in marker and have bright papers than erase in pencil and have dull perfect ones. Not until your child is regularly editing and wants to erase are pencils the best tools.

Minimarkers, such as the one in illustration 6, are extremely popular with young children. About five inches in length, minimarkers are the ideal size for tiny fingers. Their ink supplies last a long time and children who are drawing or writing can see around their writing tool to observe their work as it progresses. You can easily carry minimarkers in your pocket to use whenever your child wants to draw or write.

Most children love crayons and coloring books. Crayons are the perfect tool for coloring. As your child learns how to

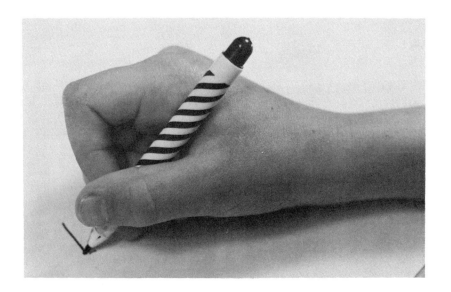

Illustration 6

write, he colors in letters that you have written and in other ways decorates writing. However, studies show that children who use coloring books a lot lose confidence in their own ability to draw things. So it is best not to introduce coloring books to your child. Of course, if a friend gives one as a present, you needn't snatch it away, but consider some alternatives. Instead of buying a coloring book, purchase a blank pad of paper. Encourage your child to draw his own pictures. Try to notice things in his pictures that will build his confidence ("Wow, your alligator certainly has big teeth!"). Such comments not only make your child feel good about drawing but also give him hints on improving the quality of his drawings without directly teaching him art.

Schools buy thick crayons and pencils for children to use because they don't break as easily as the regular size. Fat crayons are more difficult to manipulate and most children don't enjoy them as much as they do the regular size.

Because your child sees you writing with pencils and ball-point pens, he will be eager to use these tools. Ball-point pens, of course, smudge badly and must be used precisely for their points to produce ink. Therefore, wait until your child is older for ink pens. Your child needs pencils with erasers. Pencils should have soft lead (#2), and a pencil sharpener needs to be within reach. Little hand-held pencil sharpeners usually work as well as large, wall-mounted ones. These little sharpeners, made of wood or plastic, come in a variety of shapes and are perfect because they can stay right at the writing table. Once they get the hang of it, children will keep every pencil in the house sharpened!

Illustration 7

You'll discover that pencils put holes into thin paper, or even thick paper if your child presses too hard. Erasing can also cause paper to tear. When your child discovers these problems, you'll want to suggest using sturdier paper and erasing less often. You can buy erasers that fit over the ends of pencils. Plastic triangular grips which fit over a pencil to facilitate a better hand position for writing are also popular.

You probably use a variety of writing tools for a variety of purposes. You use ball-point pens when writing in your check book, pencils for arithmetic, and felt-tip pens when making out your shopping lists. Your children enjoy having the same options.

Colored pencils need to be of very soft lead; most of the ones readily available in stores are not! It is best to buy colored pencils in art supply stores. Since colored pencils are best for shading and more subtle coloring, they are easier for older children to use. The same can be said for oil-based crayons, which have brillant colors, but can smear and smudge and are most appropriately used for color blending. Charcoal, because of its messiness, is another medium you will want to wait to try with your older child.

Colored chalk and white chalk are necessary for chalkboards. However, you can use large pieces that don't break easily on paper as well. Dark construction paper takes light-colored chalk rather well.

Most children love to paint. For some, the messier the paints are, the better! An easy way to set your child up to paint is to buy containers of dry tempera paint in the basic colors red, yellow, and blue. Add white to make lighter shades and you'll find that your child can mix almost any color from these four. When you set out the paints, put some of each dry color in a little container like a baby food jar. Place near these jars a can of water, a moist sponge, some paintbrushes, and a pallet. (Plastic lids make excellent pallets.)

Teach your child how to dip his paintbrush in water, then in dry paint, then blot it on the sponge, and put the paint on the pallet. He can put several colors on the pallet at a time and mix them before painting from the pallet to the paper. This method works better than mixing paints ahead of time, for three reasons. Since you can't accurately estimate how much of each color your child will use, if you mix paints ahead of time, a lot of paint will be wasted. By mixing his own colors on the pallet, your child is learning a lot about color and tone, making his pictures more creative. And, using the sponge and pallet, the paint is not as running and uncontrollable as wet paints are likely to be.

At first, your child's primary interest is in mixing the colors. Not until he has mixed several times will he pay any attention to what he is painting on paper. By age three, most children can manage this technique.

If you mix paint for younger children, be sure it is thick enough so that it won't run. Paint is less likely to run if your child paints on a table rather than on an easel or wall. Put a drop of liquid detergent in the paint so that it will come out of clothing more easily.

Watercolor paint sets are fun for older children, but can be frustrating for very young ones who like bright colors and can't manipulate the small brushes. Color blending and shading, which watercolor does so well, is too difficult for very little children.

Your basic collection of writing tools, then, consists of minimarkers, marker pens, large-size markers, crayons, pencils with erasers, paint, and chalk. For older children, you provide oil-based crayons, soft-lead colored pencils, watercolor paints, and charcoal.

Your child, like you, enjoys having a choice of writing and drawing tools. Crayons are more appropriate for coloring, minimarkers are better for writing, and chalk is better for chalkboards. It is important to dispose of pencil stubs, dried up markers, and crayon bits (though these can be used for craft projects). Good quality writing tools will encourage your child to draw and write frequently.

Accessories

The main reason your child will give for not writing or drawing is that he can't find his "stuff." You'll need to plan with him how to store materials at his writing center. Low shelves near the center are a necessity, as are boxes, tins, and cartons of various sizes for the storage of writing tools and accessories. Together you can cover tin cans with self-sticking paper or fabric to make your center more attractive.

What other materials make writing appealing for your child? The most essential accessories are those that promote communication. Your child enjoys having his own supply of envelopes (colored ones are favored over white ones), stamps, and return address stickers. The latter can be purchased through mail order catalogs for a very small fee. If your child has to ask you for envelopes, stamps, and writing tools, he cannot be an independent writer. But if he has his own supply of these essentials, he'll more readily write on his own.

Another item your child would enjoy is an address book. You can make one by notching the sides of a small, inexpensive notebook and writing the alphabet on pages throughout the book. You might place the addresses of relatives and friends in the address book. When your child has written a letter, he can seal it in an envelope, stamp it, attach a return address sticker, and bring it to you with the address book for addressing. Your older children address their own letters. The address book also helps young children learn how to alphabetize as they search out the addresses that they need.

Your child might want an aid to spelling—either word cards for words he uses frequently, or his own spelling dictionary. Most children prefer either to ask an adult how to spell or, when an adult is unavailable, invent their own spellings. Spelling is discussed in another chapter but, for some children in some stages of their development, word cards, homemade dictionaries, or published children's dictionaries are appropriate accessories for a writing center.

Your child may also need a model of the alphabet taped to his writing table as a handy reference. Children who are just learning how to form letters or children who are making the transition to cursive appreciate having a model of the alphabet on hand. It is best to obtain the model from your child's teacher at school to provide consistency.

In addition to all the accessories which promote communication, you'll want some accessories which promote experimentation with writing. Children love to use scissors. Cutting with scissors helps develop small muscle control, which, in turn, helps prepare your child for handwriting. Purchase good quality, sharp scissors with rounded points. There is nothing more frustrating to a child than not being able to cut something out because the scissors are dull. Also, if your child is left-handed, it is important to purchase left-handed scissors.

You'll want to supervise your child's first use of scissors to prevent trimmed hair and clothing. After your child can clearly discriminate between what is appropriate for cutting and what is not, you can add scissors to the center. It is important, also, not to push a young child into cutting with scissors before he has the small muscle control to cut with ease. Tearing is easier and helps small children use their muscles before they are ready to cut. Your child needs a lot of practice tearing bits of paper before you present him with scissors.

If your child likes to cut, he may also be fond of pasting. Glue is easier to use than paste, but the texture of white paste requires the use of a brush or stick, giving children more involvement with the pasting process. Your child will love to have his own dispenser for clear adhesive tape. Other accessories, such as rulers and compasses, become useful when your child measures things. And for children who like to make things pretty, you can find gummed stickers in a variety of decorative patterns.

You can rotate many of these accessories in and out of the writing center as interest rises and wanes. Clearly, with this amount of material, storage and organization are necessary. If your child's writing table is cluttered, it will be difficult to find needed materials and little time will be spent at the center.

Illustration 8

Displaying Children's Artwork and Writing

In addition to providing a place and materials for the creation of artwork and writing, it is important to provide places to display your child's work. A bulletin board near the writing center is ideal for writing notes or reminders and for displaying postcards, greeting cards, and letters that your child has received.

One young child, not yet a reader, received a Valentine which his mother tacked up on his bulletin board. The child pulled his mother to the bulletin board repeatedly and asked to have the card read to him. Finally, he memorized the message and eagerly brought all visitors to the bulletin board to "read" the message to them. Bulletin boards then, can enhance reading as well as writing.

Your bulletin boards can also display writing and artwork that the child has done in school. In your home you might frame and hang exceptionally good pieces. If your child sees that his work is valued, he will be eager to produce more of it. Bulletin board displays should be changed frequently so that you all don't become tired of them. When you change your bulletin board, you might ask your child if he might like to store old artwork in a special file.

Providing Time for Writing

Television, radios with earphones, and many recreational opportunities compete with reading and writing for children's time. Just as you would not expect your child to become a pianist without daily piano practice or a good reader without daily reading sessions, you cannot expect your child to be an accomplished writer without a great deal of practice. Fitting writing time into your family's daily schedule is the answer.

One family sets aside a daily writing time when each member of the family writes—parents included. Parents serve as models when they participate with their children. Right after supper, everyone in this family writes, with no limits set on what is written. One child keeps a personal diary; another is writing and refining poems for his own poetry collection; and a third writes letters to grandparents and friends. The parents use this time to catch up on correspondence as well.

In addition to routine times for writing, your child can work on special writing projects, such as making Valentines and creating books as gifts. Scheduling times for writing and providing extended time for specific projects give writing the prominence in family activities that it deserves.

Chapter 3

Scribblers

"**D**at's not a scwibble. It says, 'What's for dinner, Mom?'"

Children are scribblers from the time they hold a writing tool until after they learn to write their names. There is a progression to their scribbles which moves from random scribbling, to controlled scribbling, to the naming of scribbling, to writing mock letters and words, to learning, finally, how to write. It is important not to underestimate the value of scribbling as a foundation for writing.

Illustration 9

Early Scribbling

Well before his first birthday, your child is ready to make marks on paper or a chalkboard. Those first marks will be random scribbles. Your child won't even be watching as he is making the mark and will not see the connection between the mark on paper and the writing tool in his hand. This first stage of development is called "uncontrolled scribbling."

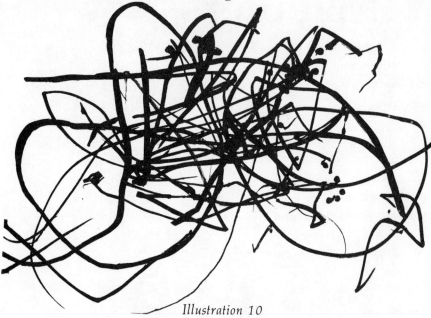

Illustration 10

The outstanding feature of these early writing attempts is that they are more than random marks; they represent your child's intentions to create something. Scribbling has been termed "gesturing with a pencil." The role of scribbling in writing development has been compared with babbling in oral language development. In each case, there is probably some random sound or scribble made but, in both cases, your child is intending to communicate.

The urge to scribble is innate. For instance, your child might scribble in the sand at the beach, in the dirt of your garden, or on a foggy car window on a rainy day. When you notice this, provide him with paper and a marker.

If you can put up with the mess, washable watercolor markers are best for early scribbling because they make marks easily in bright, clear colors. Crayons need more pressure to produce dark colors. Thick chalk on a sturdy chalkboard, however, is another perfect medium for your beginning scribbler.

Of course, your child's fingers also make excellent scribbling "tools." You can make finger paint that is washable by mixing tempera paint, Ivory Flakes, and water. Occasionally, preschoolers finger paint with materials like chocolate pudding. Toddlers who lick pudding from their fingers have a hard time determining why they cannot lick fingerpaint off as well.

Your child may be far more interested in the process of making scribbles than in the product produced by those scribbles. You, however, may want to write your child's name in the corner of the picture, letting him watch as you write. As scribble pictures get framed, mounted or displayed, your youngster soon learns that his scribble pictures are valued. He will want to draw more, not only because scribbling is so innately pleasurable but also because his scribbling attracts your positive attention.

Don't ask your child what his scribbles are. The scribbles at this stage do not represent anything. Rather, comment on what is apparent—lines from top to bottom or across the page, dots, and colors. You might say, "I like your orange and brown picture," or "What beautiful blue lines!"

Your young child watches when you write. He enjoys "helping" write the weekly grocery list. Though tiny children don't understand the meaning of the writing, they can pick up a lot just from watching you. They learn that you can read what you write and that marks on a piece of paper have meaning. This concept takes a long time to develop, but you can help by writing with your child.

Controlled Scribbling

Gradually, after much playing around with markers, chalk, and crayons, your child's scribbles become more controlled. He begins to see the relationship between the marks he is making on paper and the writing utensil in his hand. His scribbles are more systematic, as in illustration 12. The lines go up and down as in illustration 11, or in circles. Dots may surround the picture, as in illustration 13. He systematically scribbles with each marker in the box, as in illustration 14. Later, as part of the scribble pattern, circles, triangles, arrows, and squares may emerge.

Illustration 11

Illustration 12

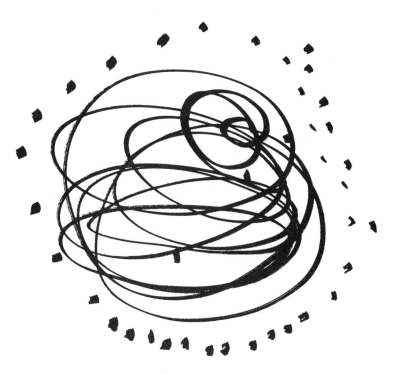

Illustration 13

Illustration 14

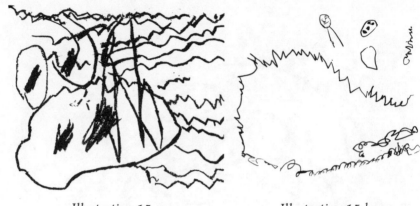

Illustration 15 a   Illustration 15 b

This is when you can expect your child to first demonstrate the difference between drawing and writing. Your child may not call his writing "writing," and it may be haphazard, but it looks different from drawing. One distinction between scribble-writing and scribble-drawing is that the former is linear, as in illustrations 15 a and b. The drawings in these illustrations are clearly distinguishable from the writing. The scribbles that represent writing take the form and shape of handwriting in whatever culture the child is from. Chinese children scribble-write vertically, while English children scribble-write horizontally. Some scribbles are more like manuscript forms, as in illustration 16 while others look like cursive writing, as in illustrations 17 a and b.

Illustration 16

Illustration 17 a

Illustration 17 b

As scribbling becomes more sophisticated, your child distinguishes among the types of writing in his scribbles. Scribble stories take on the form of a story with titles and, sometimes, even an indented first paragraph. Scribble letters and notes always have signatures. Some authors cite this phenomenon as evidence that children learn to write from whole texts down to words, then to alphabet letters, instead of the reverse. Scribbling, then, is far more complex than most people realize, and it serves a central function in the development of both drawing and writing.

Scribbles, like babbles, often are repeated. This rehearsal process represents your child's self-initiated drill and active thought with regard to the scribbles that are being produced. Often, there is a tie to oral language as the child pretends that the scribbles are actual writing.

Scribbling also develops small muscles, helping your child to gain better control of the writing tool. It doesn't matter how he holds the tool. Not until he begins to write will the grip change for writing, and that change will come about naturally. In the meantime, scribbling is giving him a great deal of practice on the "basic strokes" of handwriting—circles, straight lines, and slanted lines.

You need to write for your child when he is in the controlled-scribbling stage. Together, you can create greeting cards and letters, with you writing a simple message and your child scribbling a picture to accompany it, as in illustration 18. He may or may not follow along visually as you write.

Illustration 18

If your child receives greeting cards, you'll want to post them on a low bulletin board where he can read them. He will learn the relationship between reading and writing by reading and reacting to other people's writings.

Naming Scribbling

When your child starts requesting labels for his drawings, he is ready for real growth in writing. The scribbles now represent something. They may not look like what he says they are, but the scribbles were created with intent. Accepting his scribbles for what they are is important.

Labels begin with one word, such as "cat" or "Mommy." Children become fascinated with labels at this stage, asking that many things be labeled: "Sally's Garage" on a garage made from blocks, or "Tom's Building" on a Tinker Toy construction, and "Ice Cream—50¢" on a Lego ice cream truck, are examples. You can make a museum out of a shelf or cardboard box for collecting things to be labeled: shells, acorns, pine cones, leaves, pebbles, and so on. You can attach labels to shelves where toys are stored: blocks, puzzles, beads, books, or records are some examples. At this stage, you need to write for your child frequently, since he cannot write for himself. Short signs provide labeling experiences. One child asked her babysitter to write a "Do Not Disturb" sign for her door, to which she added, "No Cats" and went to bed for her nap. Another child requested a "wet paint" sign for a painting. Children at this stage want notes, messages, greeting cards, or postcards written for them.

Your child may exhibit a progression of behaviors while dictating to you. At first, he may not watch while you write. Placing him on your lap helps focus attention on the act of writing. Gradually he will progress through these stages:

- Watches while words are being written.
- Displays audience awareness (instead of "tell her I love her," the child says, "I love you").
- Paces dictation to the speed of the writer.
- Attempts to read what is written.
- Attempts to write (or copy) parts of the message.

These latter behaviors occur during the beginning writing stage.

At the naming scribbling stage, your child may discover alphabet letters in his scribbles and then begin to try to form them correctly. Children pretend-write whole stories, just as prior to reading, children "read" by making up words for any print they see. This "romancing" paves the way for copying and the appearance of mock letters.

Scribbles are repeated and elaborated upon. Usually children give scribble-writing symbols names. One child called cursive-like scribbles "wankushanes," and manuscript-like scribbles (sticks) "OE's." Another child called all of his letter-like forms his "DC's."

As your child scribble-writes and plays with writing you do for him, he will trace over alphabet letters and color them in. This play with written language serves a function similar to children's play with oral language (rhyming and riddling). It develops an awareness of writing—how the alphabet letters are formed, their sizes, shapes, and relationships. And much like an adult's doodling, it provides a break from trying to form alphabet letters.

Illustration 19 shows linear scribbles. As you can see, these children were beginning to be aware that writing moves across a line. If your child reads her scribbles as a message, she understands that marks on paper communicate a message. The child

Illustration 19

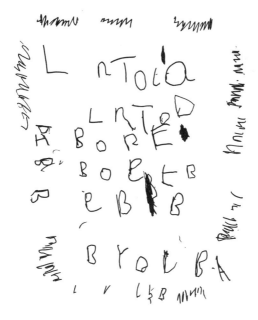

Illustration 20

who wrote illustration 20 used alphabet letters from her name as well as **A** and **B,** which she had been taught in school. This time, her cursive wiggles decorate the margins of her paper. She has clearly separated her cursive and manuscript symbols. In this case, manuscript symbols may be in the center because those are the ones she is closest to reading, while the cursive are outside because those are more difficult to read. Studying your child's scribbles will give you insight into your child's thoughts about writing.

Learning to Write a Name

When your child names his scribbles, he begins to copy your writing, especially if you have been labeling his pictures. At the same time, he may ask you to teach him how to write his name. You can teach your child to write his name by writing it so he can see you form the letters. If you call each alphabet letter out loud as you write it, he'll learn to divide the word into its letter parts. If you've done this since he was tiny, your child already knows the names of the alphabet letters which form his name. You should write in clear manuscript printing in lowercase letters (except for the first one). The manuscript alphabet is found in Appendix A at the back of this book. It is wise, however, to obtain a model from the elementary school that your child will attend, if this is possible.

As your child is learning to write his name, you'll want to have models on his writing and drawing table for him to copy when you are not around. Be careful not to criticize his initial efforts at writing, no matter how they look. Perfect letter formation comes much later.

Resist the temptation to provide your child with stencils, templates, or dotted letters to trace. When tracing, your child is only thinking of how to stay on the line; when copying, the thought process is far more complex—how to form the letter. This more advanced thinking helps him become an independent writer sooner. Tracing also slows down and inhibits a child's formation of basic strokes.

You might worry about your child if he practices writing his name incorrectly. There is, however, considerable research which indicates that children continue their efforts to approximate perfection when given consistent models of handwriting or spelling. What this means is that each time your child writes a name, he is newly rethinking the formation and spacing of each alphabet letter.

Practicing writing a name is boring and meaningless unless it is child-initiated. Instead, suggest that the child write greeting cards, notes, and personal letters, all of which require his signature. Nametags or placecards for the table are always fun to make. Learning to write one's name can take a long time. Children who learn how to write their names gradually, as part of meaningful communication, learn more easily than those who are pushed by their parents to write them. Unless children see reasons for writing their names, there is no sense in teaching that skill.

Name development typically progresses as follows:
- scribbling a name.
- writing a name in mock letters.
- copying a name.
- writing a name that is illegible.
- writing a first name legibly, but misspelled.
- writing a first name correctly with some letter reversals.

- writing a first name correctly.
- writing a first name with last initials.
- writing a first and last name legibly and correctly spelled.

Alphabet Letter Awareness

Long before children begin writing, they are developing letter awareness. They are not only learning the names of the alphabet letters, but also their shapes and how they are formed. Letter awareness also includes the functions of letters within words.

Young children learn to recognize alphabet letters through their many encounters with writing—by being read to, by writing, through their manipulative play with alphabet letters, and by observing print in the environment. The labels on grocery products, store signs, T.V., street signs, the logos for fast-food restaurants, and toys all give children daily exposure to alphabet letters. Alphabet books and "Sesame Street" also provide exposure to letters in isolation as well as in words.

Letter awareness begins when children find alphabet letters in their environment. One child asked her dad what the letter O was in an alphabet book. On her walk around the block the next day, she approached the STOP sign and exclaimed, "O!" instead of her customary, "Stop!" The following day, she was dialing a play telephone when she discovered another O. Not long after this, O's began appearing in her scribble pictures.

Young children announce with glee when they discover alphabet letter forms in their scribbles. For example, in illustration 21, one little girl called her scribble picture, "an M with an apron." Children try to repeat a form over and over again. They comment that alphabet letters look like other familiar shapes. One child thought his string of W's resembled waves; his S's were snakes; and H was a window.

If you discuss shapes with your child, this may lead to differentiation between large letters and small ones, and to differentiation between uppercase and lowercase letters. A child whose parents wrote mainly in lowercase letters noticed that his dad had written an uppercase E on his Easter card. This gave the father an opportunity to talk with his child about why some letters are capitalized and some are not. Your child will

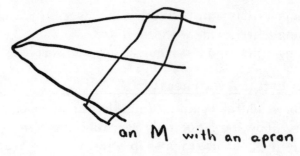

an M with an apron

Illustration 21

invent his own system of capitalization, using uppercase letters for important words or words with strong meaning for him. Initially, he may write whichever is easier to form. Uppercase **H, E, F, M,** and **Q** seem easier to form than their lowercase counterparts. To keep from confusing lowercase **b** and **d,** some children tend to write uppercase forms of those letters. Encourage your child to experiment in this way. He can refine letter forms and learn capitalization rules after he can write well.

Not only do children need to be able to recognize alphabet letters in order to write them, but they also need to understand how those alphabet letters are formed. There are over ten ways an uppercase **A** can be written with three strokes (more if it is thought of as having five strokes). How does your child learn, for example, to make letter strokes from the top downward? This is where your modeling by writing for your child is essential.

Word Awareness

Word awareness begins as does alphabet-letter awareness, with the recognition of words in the environment: Stop, Bus Stop, Safeway, Sesame Street, and Walk are some examples. At this time, children begin to differentiate between words and alphabet letters. Their talk while composing indicates this developing awareness. They'll ask an adult to make an alphabet letter but expect the adult to write a word for them. You can help your child learn that white spaces separate words by leaving spaces between words as you write for him and by keeping the letters within words relatively close together. The child will recognize individual words when you point to each word as you read what you have written for him.

Illustration 22 a   Illustration 22 b

Illustration 22 c

Illustration 22 d

One can see evidence of children's development of word boundaries when they place markers other than white spaces between words. Illustrations 22 a-d show word awareness at several different levels. Ryan (a) has encircled his scribbles, with one word on each line, except for what looks like an **I**. Donelle (b) circles her mock words which contain some alphabet letters and some mock letters. Skye (c) boxes in each word in her message to her parents. Jonathan (d) on the other hand, places periods as word markers in his story.

Another part of word awareness is spelling awareness, which will be described in more detail in Chapter Seven. Your child begins to notice that several words begin the same way or end with the same alphabet letter. He finds little words in big ones and plays with words to change them into new words. He realizes that there is consistency to the written word: "Dog," for example, is always spelled the same, as are many other words.

Some of the first words children want to learn to read and write are names—their names first, then the names of other family members, pets, friends, and favorite storybook characters. Names stand out in most reading material because of their uppercase beginnings, and they are excellent devices for developing word awareness in children.

Other words that are noticed early on are words that have some emotional content or special meaning for the child. In her book *Teacher*, (Simon & Schuster, 1971) Sylvia Ashton-Warner calls these "key words." "Ice cream," "watermelon," "Halloween," and "I love you," are examples.

The distinction between words and alphabet letters is a critical one for reading development. Nowhere is that distinction more obvious than in learning to write.

Writing Awareness

There are many conventions of writing that are arbitrary and peculiar to the English language. Writing moves from left to right, then back to the left at the end of a line, from top to bottom on a page, and then back to the left when you turn the page. Spaces appear between words, and punctuation aids readers in interpreting messages. The principal concept behind writing awareness is that graphic symbols have meaning. Learning to read or write is immeasurably more difficult if children lack this basic knowledge about writing.

Two factors greatly assist your child in learning writing

awareness. The first factor is present when you write for him so that he can see you generate a message. As he repeatedly observes the conventions of writing "in action," he may copy those models and think about them. His thoughts help him acquire writing awareness.

The second factor that helps a child learn writing awareness is play with written language. After you have written for him, your child will play with the writing by coloring in the letters or tracing over them. Although teaching him to form alphabet letters by having him trace is usually inappropriate (as will be explained in Chapter Six), his play-tracing of alphabet letters, when he initiates it, serves a most useful function in the development of writing awareness.

Your child learns a great deal during play because he thinks as he plays. Just as he plays with oral language ("silly, Billy, nilly, dilly"), he needs to play with written language. Further, he will enjoy playing with writing. Some kindergarten children retrieved an experience chart which their teacher had thrown away, and played with it. They circled alphabet letters, underlined words, drew pictures, colored in letters, traced some writing, and generally studied all aspects of the message. What a lot they learned from playing with that discarded chart!

A young child, whose parents had written many personal letters for her, dictated "Dear Aunt Jean," when sending her aunt a Valentine. This child was very aware of the format for a personal letter; so familiar, in fact, that she could not switch to the greeting card format of "Happy Valentine's Day." When another child first wrote his own personal letters, he automatically indented the body of the letters, as he'd seen his dad do so often when writing for him. For each kind of writing, there are special characteristics that children learn through watching adult models.

Writing awareness, then, involves acquiring information about written language. It links oral and written language and is often neglected in our push toward teaching children to read or write.

Audience Awareness

When young children are dictating, drawing, and writing real messages for other people, they quickly become aware of audiences for their writing. After a parent suggested that a child "draw a picture for Grandma" and the child saw his drawing attached to Grandma's wall a few days later, he returned to draw many more pictures "for Grandma" and any other adult who praised his creations.

By listening to children as they compose, adults can determine audience awareness. Terry said, "I'm making this one green because green is Kelly's favorite color." Terry was aware that his card would be more appreciated by his brother if it were written in green. Amy commented, "Won't Santa like my letter in red and green Christmas colors?" She, too, was aware that the communication was for someone.

Since the communications of children often receive responses, children themselves become an audience for writing. They experience firsthand what it is like to receive communication, which gives them a different perspective on audience awareness. After receiving a thank you note for a baby gift, one child read the message over and over to his babysitter and other visitors to the home. The card was tacked on his bulletin board to be shared with everyone.

Audience awareness helps your child make sense out of writing. Why would he want to learn how to make a letter **D,** or write the word "Dear," unless he were in the process of writing a letter to someone? Sometimes, he may write for himself as an audience. And, sometimes, his audience can be distant—as when writing a book. But most often he will want to communicate with those who are closest to him.

Chapter 4

Beginning Writers

"The Rezin I Rote Th's becuz . . ."
"Want's apana TIM . . ."

Children progress from learning how to write their names, where handwriting is a slow and labored process, to being able to write anything they want rather quickly with little thought given to handwriting. Learning to write can be an exciting adventure, filled with lots of experimentation and play with language. Unfortunately, it can also be tedious and boring if the child is forced to copy meaningless alphabet letters one at a time. One child was asked by her nursery school teacher to connect dots to form the letter l. She was given an entire page of these to do. She dutifully made line after line of l's but her boredom broke through and she rebelled. On the last line—she made only o's! It is your role as a parent to ensure that your child realizes writing is for communication and that there is always a receptive audience for early writing efforts.

The Transition from Scribbling To Writing

Children may learn how to write their names while they are still scribbling. As scribbles take on the semblance of manuscript and cursive writing, shapes and designs—which are called mock letters—begin to appear.

Mock letters can be symmetrical, like the alphabet letters **A, H, I, M, O, T, U, V, W,** and **X** (illustration 23).

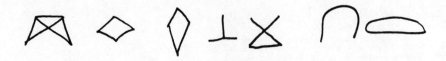

Illustration 23

Mock letters can have interiors and exteriors, like the alphabet letters, **A, B, D, O, P, Q,** and **R.**

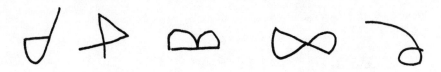

Illustration 24

Mock letters can have intersections like **A, E, F, H, J, K, L, M, N, Q, R, T, V, W, X,** and **Z.**

Illustration 25

They can have exterior dots like **i** and **j.**

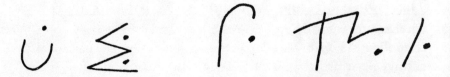

Illustration 26

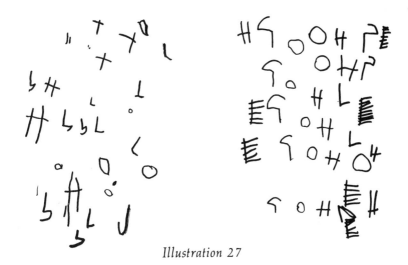

Illustration 27

Your child may begin to draw mock letters linearly from left to right across the page. In illustration 27 you can see the letters in Shontell's name begin to appear more clearly as he moves from writing all over the page to writing linearly. If a child knows that the white spaces between words are word boundaries, he'll cluster his letter shapes into mock words as Javonette has done in illustration 28.

Illustration 28

Children's scribbles, drawings, and mock writing display several interesting principles and concepts about beginning writers. These are described by Marie Clay in a book called *What Did I Write?* (Heinemann Educational Books, 1975.) The first concept children learn is the "sign concept." They are aware that certain symbols carry a message. They see lots of signs in their environment. Children use mock letters to make signs and strings of **xxx**'s and **ooo**'s for kisses and hugs.

Children acquire a "message concept" when they realize that what they say can be written down. You help your child develop a "message concept" when you write for him or attempt to read something he has written. (Tactfully responding to reading your child's "message" is an art you will need to acquire.)

The Copying Principle

Most children, at one point or another, copy adult writing. Since copying is so tedious, most children rapidly discard it and begin to invent their own ways to write. Sometimes, children trace over what an adult has written or copy underneath the adult's message. These copying and tracing behaviors serve to help youngsters check on how well they are developing the ability to write. Most children, at one time or another, write the words to a song or something else they have memorized. They enjoy seeing what something familiar looks like in writing.

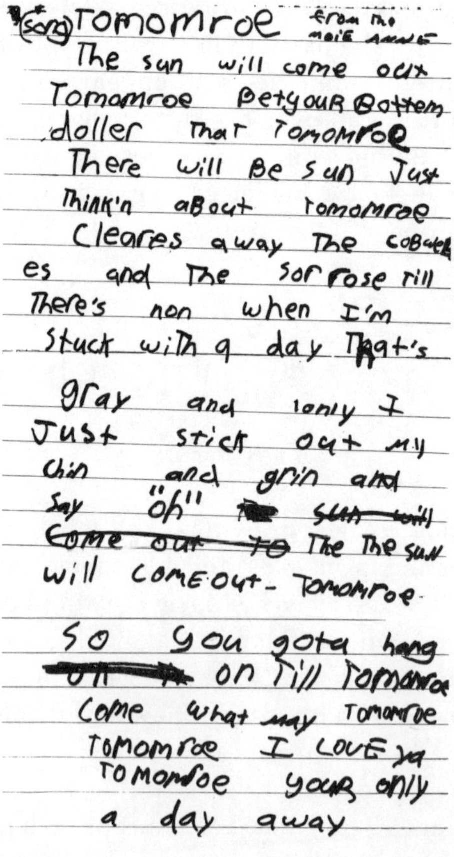

Illustration 29

The Flexibility Principle

Children use the flexibility principle to test out their concepts of writing. As they play with writing by reversing letters, moving them around the page, alternating letters within words, and alternating the spellings of words, they learn how inflexible the written message really is. Much advanced thinking accompanies play with writing. Words which once were spelled correctly become misspelled. There is a parallel to speech development where children who once used correct past tenses now use overgeneralized past tenses ("runned") as they become more flexible in their oral language.

The Inventory Principle

Children enjoy writing what they know. At the beginning writing stages, what they know can be inventoried on lists. At this stage, your child may make lists of the people he knows, his babysitters, friends, foods, animals, and any other words he can write. He'll inventory the alphabet letters he can form. In illustrations 30 a-d, Josi (a) lists all the Spanish words she can write; Earl (b) lists all the **-ay** words he can think of; and David (c) lists the musical alphabet. At a later stage, stories become lists of sentences, as in illustration 31. And Olivia's story about the Care Bears in illustration 32 is really an inventory.

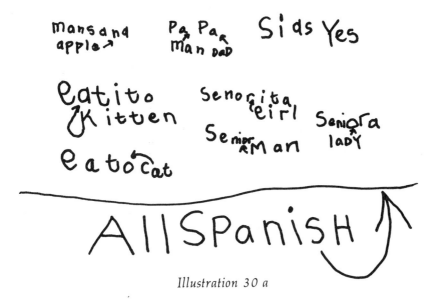

Illustration 30 a

Day Zay Pay
Hay Bay Lay
May tay Cay
Ray

Do
Ra
Me
Fa
So
La
Te
Do

Illustration 30 b   *Illustration 30 c*

I like mom
I like DaD
I like Me
I like Julie
I like you
~~I like~~ I like E. T.

Illustration 31

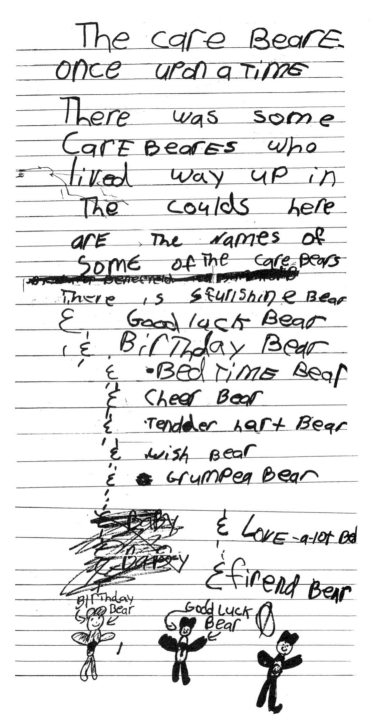

The care BearE.
once upon a TimE

There was some
CarE BeareS who
lived way up in
The coulds here
are The names of
Some of the care bears

There is sEunShine Bear
& Good luck Bear
& BirThday Bear
& Bed Time Bear
& Cheer Bear
& Tendder hart Bear
& wish Bear
& Grumpea Bear

& LovE-a-lot Bd
& firend Bear

BirThday
Bear
Good Luck
Bear

Illustration 32

The Recurring Principle

Repetition is self-initiated drill for young children. In both drawing and writing, they repeatedly draw the same forms and write the same messages. Each time, they are mastering the form and gaining precision in their graphic depiction. At this stage, your child may accompany each message with an exclamation point, a heart, or a star. His messages may say, "I love you. I miss you." His stories may begin, "Once upon a time . . . " Most children repeat certain forms of writing, such as messages, over and over again (To: Mom, From: Jim). In illustrations 33 a-c, children at different levels of writing ability demonstrate the recurring principle using mock letters (a), words (b), and messages (c).

Illustration 33 a

Illustration 33 b

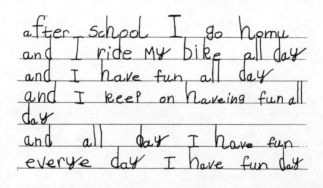

Illustration 33 c

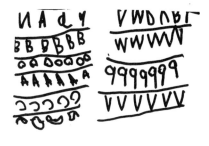

Illustration 34 a   Illustration 34 b

The Generating Principle

Children begin with a simple form, alphabet letter, or message and then expand it as they generate new patterns for writing. They write alphabet letters in rows while generating new letters on the end of strings. In illustrations 34 a and b, two children have generated new alphabet letter forms.

Words begin in their simplest forms (Mom) until they later appear as more complete forms (Mommy). Writing develops as children write their first names, then their first and last names, and then their entire first, middle, and last names. The generating principle is very evident in different forms of writing. For example, your child may compose friendly letters consisting of the necessary elements: the greeting, a few sentences in the body, and a closing, but drawings may be used to take up the rest of the space. Gradually, he learns to generate more context. For example, the beginning letter might say, "Dear Sue, I love you. I miss you. Love, Dan." A later form would repeat this message, but add something to it. "Dear Sue, I love you. I miss you. Rascal had puppies. Love, Dan." Still later forms would repeat the initial sentences but add to them, "How are you?" or other phrases common in friendly letters. A last way of expanding the letter repertoire is to add a P. S., which often says, "Write soon."

The Directional Principles

Besides learning that writing moves from left to right, your child must also learn that when one line is completed, he must return to the left margin. These directional principles become easier to master as children learn to read. In the meantime, the flexibility principle will help your child solve directional problems, especially what to do when he runs out of space at the end of a paper. Until your child can plan ahead and leave space for what he writes, directional problems will be encountered. He may solve these by moving up and around the edge of the paper, or down and around the edge of the paper; he may return from right to left on a line above or below the original one and use arrows to indicate where the next segment of text appears.

Illustration 35

In illustration 35, Dhruva happened to begin the alphabet in the lower left-hand corner of the page. Except for the **J,** which is formed with a right-to-left stroke, Dhruva wrote her letters in the correct direction when writing across the bottom of the page and up the side. Only when writing from right to left across the top does Dhruva make reversals. The letters **DREUOQ** represent Dhruva's name and were added at the end.

Kenyata made a similar reversal of the letter **a** on her card to Tamara as she began writing from right to left in illustration

Illustration 36

36. When she realized she was writing backwards, she inserted the final **n** between the **l** and the **a**. She didn't like the looks of this card, so began over again on a new sheet of paper. In illustration 37, Marah used the flexibility principle, the directional principle, and the contrastive principle in creating mirror images of her message, "To Nora." Adrienne's mirrored

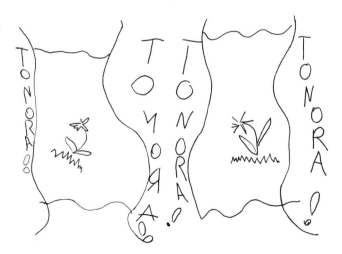

Illustration 37

repetitions of her name in illustration 38 include reversals of **E, r, n, D** and lowercase **e.** In most cases, these correspond to the direction she was writing at the time. Reversals and mirror writing are common as children work with directional principles.

Illustration 38   Illustration 39

The Contrastive Principle
Young children need to explore the world of writing and try to make sense out of it. One way they do this is by systematically putting their knowledge in order. The contrastive principle is a method of organizing knowledge. Some alphabet letters invite comparisons (**b** and **d; g** and **p; u** and **n; m** and **w**). Words invite comparison (big and little, boy and girl, tall and short, loud and soft). There are upper and lowercase alphabet letters to contrast. There are color and size contrasts evident as children begin to write. There may be directional contrasts as well. The content of your child's writing at early stages often includes contrastive elements. For example, he may contrast what he likes with what he does not like; or what makes him happy and what makes him sad.

Illustration 39 is an example of the contrastive principle. In her list of letters, Sylvia has contrasted upper and lowercase letter **b,** uppercase **A** and **V** forms, and a backwards **C** and upside-down **U** contrast the position of the curve. **P** becomes an **R,** while the **L** and **r** are mirror images of each other, as are the **W** and **M** at the end.

Early Writing and Drawing: Some Relationships

The scribbles that are named on a child's drawing gradually become recognizable shapes. The same shapes form the foundation for both drawing and writing. Circles and lines combine as they become people and animals with arms, legs, facial features, and even belly buttons! These drawings have no relationship to each other, appearing haphazardly on the page. Sometimes the child changes the item being drawn several times before it is complete. What starts as a bug may become a car and then a fire truck.

Illustration 40

These basic shapes become alphabet-letter forms. Children attempt to repeat those letters, which at first randomly appear in scribbles. They attempt to create letters they have seen repeatedly, such as those in their names. Many times, letters come out backwards or upside down; and, like drawings, the letters appear randomly over the page. Alphabet letters at this point are thought of by children more as objects of art than of writing. They claim to "make" an **A** or "draw" a **P,** but they "write" a story. The distinction between alphabet letters (linked to both drawing and handwriting) and messages (which have meaning) is reflected in their talk as they write. Gradually, writing and drawing become distinct as each begins to carry a message in a different form.

The parallels between writing and drawing are particularly strong at this stage. Just as drawings wander all over the page, so does writing. Even after your child understands left-right directionality and top-bottom orientation, if there is no room on the paper, the remainder of the work or message is as likely to go up as it is to go down.

Your child's early writings are frequently labels for drawings that are scattered around the page. He may enjoy making arrows from his labels to his pictures.

Early labeled pictures are static, even if they depict actions.

WSCRS AR ON HiSFAS

Illustration 41

Gradually your child will progress to the next stage of drawing, where stereotyped pictures begin to appear: grass, sky, and a house with smoke coming from the chimney. These schematic drawings are not as interesting or as pretty to the adult eye as earlier ones. At this level, however, the picture is an integrated whole. The elements in it relate to one another.

If children draw pictures before they write, as beginning writers typically do, their writing has to fit around their pictures.

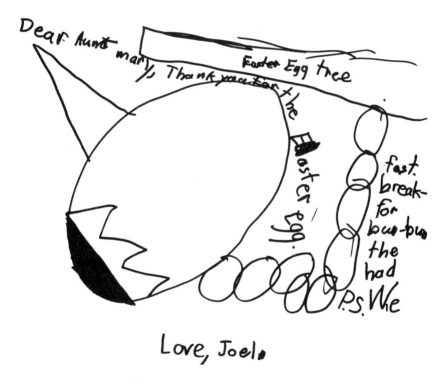

Illustration 42

Later, schematic drawings become more dynamic when children leave space to "tell about what is happening" in them. In this way, writing helps their drawing abilities mature. Illustration 43 shows not only a picture with writing planned to "show" something, but also schematic drawings with some action in them. Encouraging children to write in the present tense

Dadis planting flowers.

Illustration 43

instead of the past tense ("Dad is planting flowers") helps bridge the gap in writing between labeling pictures and telling a story as well as make the transition from static schematic drawings to dynamic ones.

In a similar fashion, labeling drawings pushes the child artist to draw with more detail. The tractor in illustration 44 was a mere outline until the child illustrator began to label its parts.

More advanced beginning artists draw action in their schematic pictures. When this occurs, people appear in profile form and the stories that accompany these pictures contain a narrative thread. Instead of a story like "This is my cat. She is black. I love my cat," stories have a plot: "My cat caught a mouse last night. She wouldn't drop it, so we had to chase her with a broom."

Illustration 44

In the beginning writing period, both drawings and texts are repeated endlessly. Once your child has perfected a schema or method for drawing a bird, a bird appears in every picture the child draws. Similarly, once your child has learned how to write, "I miss you," that phrase appears in every letter he writes. Do not underestimate the value of repetition in children's progress. One mother counted the number of "I Love You" messages that were written by Tasha when she was a beginning writer. There were well over one hundred of them. They appeared in notes and in personal letters that she had written. Repeating a form in artwork or in writing develops children's confidence and leaves children free to master new forms or alter old ones. It is helpful for you to allow and support this repetition when it is child-initiated; but you wouldn't want to drill your child in particular letters or messages.

Characteristics of Beginning Writing

Independent writing may begin as your child is labeling his drawings. He can already write his name, so he writes it everywhere. He may sign scribble notes or drawings or place his name on labels in many different places. Two little children cut up their parents' old Christmas cards, then attached them to a kitchen door with tape. As they finished each one, they signed their names on a strip of paper next to the picture. There are many opportunities to sign names, and beginning writers explore all of them.

Your child may enjoy learning how to write other people's names. Placecards for a table are useful for practicing family names. Sometimes children will make lists of words they can write. An early list is usually made up of the names of family members, pets, and friends. Later lists include shopping lists, word families (lay, say, bay, day), and simple words they can write. Lists are a good way to practice writing individual words.

In a similar fashion, beginning writers label their pictures, toys, and other creations. One-word captions are easy to write. Signs are another short form of early writing: you can tell in illustration 45 that Brian has noticed the scoreboard and the labels of the Gator football team in the university city where he lives.

Illustration 45

In addition to writing independently, beginning writers enjoy copying. Some beginning writers have been known to go to a book, such as an encyclopedia, and copy something out of it verbatim. In their eagerness to practice their newfound writing skill, children may copy entire texts from whatever written material is in their environment. One child copied definitions from a dictionary. Others have been known to copy recipes, phone numbers, and magazine titles.

Illustration 46

In illustration 46, Latasha copied a song title from "The White House Version" of an Annie record. She invented spellings even as she copied from the record cover, which shows that she was thinking about the content of the song she was writing rather than about precise copying. While you will not want to encourage copying from a book, if your child initiates the copying, you won't want to discourage it either.

Illustration 47

At this stage, children enjoy talking about their pictures. "This is a fire truck and this is a flower and this is me." You can write short statements about the drawings such as "Daddy likes orange juice" in illustration 47. If you leave space your child can copy the message if he wants to. Children learn how to correctly form alphabet letters by copying, tracing, coloring in, and otherwise playing with adult writing as well as their own writing.

At first, children usually write alphabet letters correctly because they are copying them and thinking carefully about how to form them. Later, as your child experiments and practices with alphabet letters, they may appear backwards or upside down. Still later, as he becomes fluent, he writes letters directionally correct. As a parent you should not correct letter formation until your child is fluent—certainly not as he is just beginning to write.

Illustration 48

In illustrations 48 and 49, two children wrote an entire letter backwards. Jess first wrote her alphabet, then a letter to her dad in perfect mirror writing. "Dear Dad, I hope you have a good time. I love you. From Jess." Erich wrote all but his name backwards. His letter reads, "Dear Santa, I hope you will bring me a lots of fun and toys. Superman. Erich." Both Jess and Erich write directionally correctly, but just this one time happened to start at the right (wrong) edge of the paper.

Similarly, your child may begin to write his name backwards, especially if he happens to begin writing at the right side of the page instead of the left side, or if the letter which begins his name begins with a right-to-left stroke (**C, G, J,** or **S**). Ignore all reversals at this point.

Little messages occur when children are beginning writers. If your child has access to a chalkboard or memo board, he may communicate back and forth with you or an older child. In school, cubbyholes provide places for teachers and children to leave each other notes. You might want to make cubbies or mailboxes to encourage note writing at home.

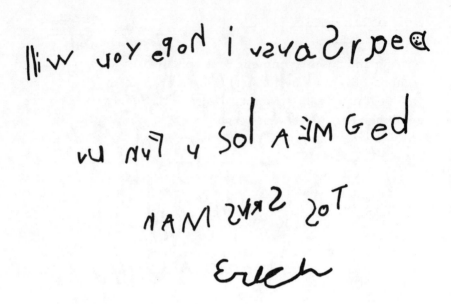

Illustration 49

Much of what beginning writers compose is merely picture doodling with interspersed words. Little scraps of paper make ideal places to doodle. Beginning writers like to cut with scissors, stick stickers, paste, draw, and write all on the same piece of paper. Sometimes, their creations take several days and a large number of sittings to complete, but a child will go back and forth from writing to other play activities.

Beginning writers are eager writers. They like to show off their accomplishments. Bulletin board displays are especially appropriate for beginning writers. Many of their works are intended to be gifts. Their pictures contain words and their writing contains pictures. Notes and messages are written to many different appreciative audiences: relatives, friends, a Sunday school teacher, the mail carrier, well-known store clerks, and anyone else the child sees regularly.

If your child is permitted to write freely from an early age, he will feel free to take risks when he is copying; confident that he knows how to spell words with which he is familiar. But children who have been confined to exact, correct copying and not allowed to experiment may copy words mindlessly, not knowing what the message is.

Role of the Adult

Your role at the beginning writing stage is to provide model writing and an environment that will encourage your child to compose. Right from the start there is a variety of writing that the beginner will attempt. There is independent writing, combined with scribbling and drawing, which constitutes play with written language. Independent writing of notes has already been discussed.

Soon, your child will want to write longer messages, either letters or stories. But writers don't write in a vacuum. The best writing is about experiences he has had. The following progression of activities can guide you as you help your beginning writer discover the challenge of composing.
1. Provide direct experience (something to write about).
2. Establish the need to communicate ("Wouldn't you like to write a book about . . . "; "How about writing to Uncle Ray and telling him about . . . "). 3. Review the experience. (Getting started is the hardest part, but rehearsal is an aspect of prewriting that makes writing much easier.) 4. Plan the writing. ("What will you say to Uncle Ray?") 5. Write and/or dictate the message. 6. Read and revise the message. (Although beginning writers cannot be expected to copy things over, they can make corrections; and they should always read what they have written.) 7. Deliver the message.

If your child is writing a story, you can help choose and review a topic so that the actual composing is easier. You may also volunteer to listen to the piece after it is written. Your role is critical, for without it, your child may never get started.

If you encourage your beginning writer to spell words as best he can and if you refrain from criticizing the spelling, you will be surprised at how quickly he moves from labeling pictures to writing long stories, and from writing safe, correctly spelled words on short notes to writing lengthy letters and messages. In one kindergarten class where children wrote freely and parents had been urged to encourage free writing, most of the children were writing long stories by the end of the year. One child wrote a note to the teacher using every line of a page of lined notebook paper. There was a lot of repetition in the message, but at the end the child said that since she had written a whole page, the teacher owed her a full page response. The teacher fulfilled the child's expectations.

Your most important role at this beginning writing stage, then, is to loosen your child from the false impression that words must be spelled correctly to be read by others and to communicate. Your child can practice invented spellings and leave learning how to spell until after he has learned how to communicate on paper. In illustration 50, J.J. has written a story of ten sentences with few words spelled conventionally, yet the message is readable: "Once there was a bear. I saw him when I was on my walk. The bear scared me. I screamed. My Mom came to check on me. Me silly. It was only my friend. I was a silly me. I like my friend a lot. I (hope) that you like my story. The end. J.J."

Illustration 50

Beginning Writing and Beginning Reading

Learning the alphabet is a meaningless task to a young child who sees no relationship between the alphabet and reading. A knowledge of the alphabet is essential for writing, however, and writing is the most natural way to develop interest in the

Growing Up Writing

alphabet. As your child learns to write, the symbols used serve an important function which he cannot fail to notice.

Writing helps your child see how words develop. Concepts of writing, such as left-right progression and visual word boundaries, are essential concepts for reading and are readily apparent in writing. By observing how language is put into writing, your youngster develops the ability to decode language.

When reading aloud, children read differently from a reading textbook than from compositions they, themselves, have written. While reading textbooks, children read word for word, as if they were reading from a list, and make few errors in their literal reading. The meaning of the passage may not be clear, and in fact, is sometimes hidden behind the correct

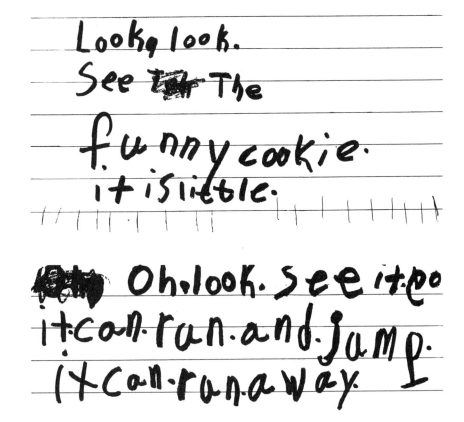

Illustration 51

naming of the words. Occasionally a child will reveal his word-for-word concept of reading in what he writes. In illustration 51, Sonya has written a "story" like the ones in her basal reader. To emphasize the word-for-word reading, she put a period after each word! Usually, when reading from their own compositions, however, children proceed right to the meaning of the passage. They read to communicate, often omitting and adding words so the message is as coherent as they can make it. In the long run, our children must read for meaning; not stopping and looking at each word, but reading phrases and even whole sentences with one eye scan. What is critical for good comprehension is getting the meaning from the written material, not pronouncing each word in the text correctly. Writing, more than reading, seems to help children read for meaning; when they're writing, children are clearly trying to communicate. It is important, then, to encourage your child to read his own compositions.

Observing Children As They Write

Adults tend to lavish praise on a child's creations—drawings, paintings, notes, greeting cards, and letters. While this praise is appropriate in most cases, it may focus your attention and that of your child on the written product rather than on the process of writing. By observing your child write, you can discover more effective ways of supporting his development.

When you observe and assist in the composing process, you gain valuable information about how your child thinks. If, for example, your child goes back and reads each individual word as he is writing, you might help by reading over his message with him to keep him progressing. If you see that he stops each time he comes to a word he can't spell, you might suggest writing down the first letter and moving on till the story is done.

Most beginning writers focus so much on the form of their writing—on letter formation, spelling, and punctuation—that they tend to lose track of where they are in their message. When you are watching carefully, you'll provide just the right amount of assistance to help him get the message out. Too little adult help results in many unfinished messages, while too much intervention prevents children from writing what they are capable of at one sitting. For beginning writers, it is better to complete a short message and to eagerly anticipate another writing experience than it is to overdo a message to make it complete in an adult's eyes.

Some children begin to write at very early ages, long before they have adequate handwriting or spelling skills. If your child is an early writer, you can write as a team, with you taking over when the child tires, as is the case in illustration 52.

Dear Kim

THank You For BABY sitting for me. I liked playing with you, especially when you were reading to me. love Nina

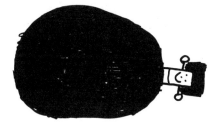

Illustration 52

Writing and Social Interaction

Some people think that writing is a lonely task, done in solitude and quiet. That may be true for adult writers, but for children, writing is a social event. In group settings, if a drawing/writing table is available, you will rarely see a child drawing or writing alone. Even at very young ages, children group themselves together to write and draw.

Children talk incessantly as they compose. They ask each other for help (especially in spelling and forming letters), plan what they are creating, rehearse their ideas, question each other about their products, share and read their work to each other, evaluate their work, and socialize. Socialization gives children a break as well as time to think and organize their compositions.

Peers provide a good support system for writing experiences. While children may get ideas from each other about what to write, or even how to write it, rarely will they simply copy each other. They'll say, "I'm going to tell about the fire, too," giving a compliment to the original author of the idea. There may be a whole "run" on cartoons or mystery stories, but each will have its own unique flavor, so you needn't be concerned about copying at the beginning writing stage.

Children in a neighborhood naturally integrate writing into their play. Signs appear on their playhouses, fire engines, and lemonade stands. Children make sheriffs' badges, tickets for special events, labels for their creations, and license plates for their bikes or trikes. At holiday times, children gather to make greeting cards and presents. Sometimes, groups of older children organize to publish a neighborhood newspaper.

You can encourage these group writing activities by organizing play groups to include writing and drawing activities. When they write in groups, children have more models. By talking together, they are "thinking out loud." Since children enjoy playing together, composing stories naturally becomes an enjoyable group activity.

How Children Are Taught to Write

Writing programs in the primary grades differ greatly among schools and even among teachers within a school. Traditional programs teach children how to form alphabet letters before they write creatively. If your child is in such a classroom, he may be asked to trace alphabet letters. Later, he copies words and sentences from a chalkboard for handwriting practice. Only after he can copy rather lengthy pieces will he have the opportunity to write on his own. At home however, he may be already writing signs, notes, messages, letters, and even stories.

You can help teachers by showing them the kinds of writing your child is doing at home. It is important for you to encourage your child to write on his own and invent spellings, or he might grow up thinking that he cannot write if he can't spell correctly. It is important, also, that your child not feel torn between what he is doing at school and what he is doing at home. You can praise his copied work while at the same time providing time and ideas for creative works at home.

Many teachers have children write frequently and invent their own spellings. Classrooms have mailboxes so children write notes to each other. In some classrooms children write in journals several times a week. If your child is in a classroom like this, you can be enthusiastic about the writings he brings home and refrain from commenting about spelling or handwriting.

The Transition to Fluency

As beginning writers become more fluent, they write faster. Writing short stories or letters does not take as long as it did previously. Alphabet letters become uniform in size and shape and children do not need to think about how each is formed. Concern with both form and content changes to concern primarily for content.

Typical of this transition period are letters such as the one in illustration 53. The letter was written independently with the exception of the word "elevator." Instead of the repetitive message, "How are you? I am fine," Laurel wrote in a more conversational tone.

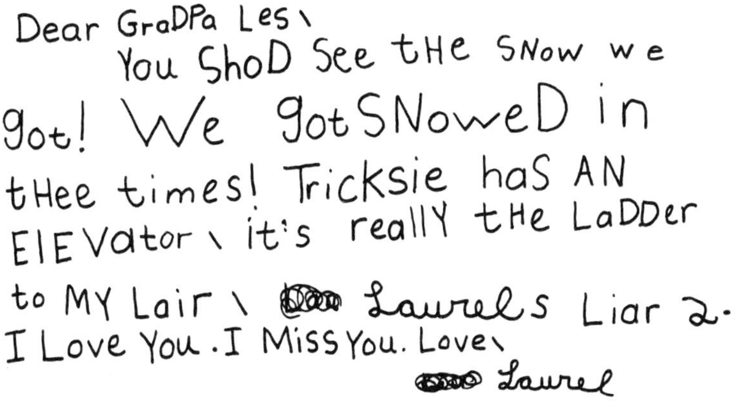
Dear GraDPa Les\
You ShoD See tHe SNow we got! We gotSNoweD in tHee times! Tricksie haS AN ElEVator\ it's reallY tHe LaDDer to MY Lair\ Laurels Liar 2.
I Love You. I MissYou. Love\
Laurel

Illustration 53

Transitional writers are beginning to punctuate their works. Laurel appropriately uses a slanted line for a comma after the greeting, after the words "elevator" and "lair," and after "love." When questioned about her punctuation, she said,

"You see, when it is not the end of the sentence, but you still have more to say, well, then, you need a line (her term for 'comma')." Exclamation points are also appropriately used. The child uses an apostrophe in "it's," though it is formed like a colon (which may have been a slip of the marker). There is no apostrophe for possession in "Laurel's."

Although the child's handwriting has evened out some in size and spacing, she is still at the beginning level because she is still capitalizing some letters that should not be capitalized (**P, D, N, H,** and **Y**). In addition, she is still capitalizing letters at the beginning of some words. This causes her writing to be slower than that of a transitional writer. It would be appropriate for a parent to recommend using lowercase alphabet letters in these places.

The transitional writer's spelling is readable. In this letter, "shod" is misspelled because of the uncommon vowel sound it contains. "Three" has an omitted blended **r.** Tricksie is spelled as trick might be and therefore is a reasonable invented spelling, very readable. The last "Lair" is merely a careless mistake, probably made because the writer was concentrating upon two more difficult tasks, writing her name in cursive and writing the numeral two.

As Laurel read this letter over, however, she recognized each of her misspellings, except Trixie, a word she probably has never seen in writing. Transitional writers recognize their spelling errors and can usually correct them. As they become ready for revision, they should learn to make corrections and copy over their drafts on a regular basis. (Personal letters are rarely copied over.)

When your child makes the transition between beginning writing and fluency, his writing changes from repetition to more mature writing. Letters become more conversational; stories begin to have more plot. Handwriting becomes more uniform and legible and faster. The child's spelling errors are rather sophisticated ones and punctuation begins to appear in appropriate locations. He also recognizes his errors and, in most cases, corrects them.

It is ironic, then, that many transitional writers tire of writing and prefer other activities. Perhaps they see for the first time that writing is more complex than it had been in the past, for they are beginning to recognize their errors. Perhaps longer pieces are more taxing; they take more time and more commitment. They take more risk, for if after spending a long time on a piece it is still not good, it may get thrown out. For whatever reason, it is at the transition between beginning writing and fluency that writers need to be urged to continue.

Your child may now be able to tell stories that are far longer and more complex than he can write by hand. For this reason, it is still important for you to take stories by dictation. At this time, your child may enthusiastically stand beside a typewriter and tell a lengthy story or letter which would otherwise not get written. He may even copy the story and illustrate it.

This transition from beginning writing to fluency is a particularly critical time for you to be sensitive to your child's needs. It is especially important not to be critical at this time, but to be supportive. One way your child may become a fluent (and faster) writer, of course, is to practice writing. But if he begins to feel that this is hard work, he will dislike writing. It is best therefore if your child continues to write when and what he desires. One parent found it helpful to suggest that her son write a letter to his grandpa to insert in the one she was writing. Writing with your child is more social and gives him a crutch for spelling, if needed. Techniques like this one, which foster writing without making it a chore, are especially helpful for children making the transition between beginning writing and fluency.

Chapter 5

Developing Fluency

"**H**ey Dad! Remember that storm we had last night? In school I wrote four whole pages about it!"
—from a family letter: "I guess I've got to go now. This ends the *longest* letter I've *ever* written. Bye, Claire. Love, Meagen."
—"Look! I'm a published author!"

When children can sit down and rather easily and quickly put their thoughts on paper, they are considered fluent writers, even if they make errors. If they are to progress, fluent writers need to write more and for a wider variety of purposes than younger writers. Many children never really attain fluency and therefore do not write for the rest of their lives. Writing a letter is torture for them, so they use the telephone instead. When asked to clerk for their club or social organization, their lack of skills becomes obvious. It is important, then, that children be encouraged and be given opportunities to become fluent writers.

Older writers engage in two types of writing: informal, which includes personal letters and diaries; and formal, which is intended for a more public audience (perhaps publication). Both types of writing should increase as the child becomes more fluent, for they each require very different types of skills.

How Children Are Taught to be Fluent in School

School programs vary widely. In some classrooms, children write once a week during a creative writing time. During these periods the children are given a topic or a choice of topics and then asked to complete a piece in half an hour. Some teachers allow children to write more frequently, while others rarely take time for children to write on their own at all. At the same time, children typically spend half an hour a day on language arts textbook worksheets where they are given directed activities, some of which may involve directed writing experiences. Children have to copy sentences and insert correct words for usage practice, or combine two sentences into one for sentence-combining. This language arts drill in skills is divorced from the writing process. Children rarely are taught how to revise their writing or how to proofread, though they may be asked to proofread their pieces before turning them in. The only audience for the writing is the teacher, who may correct the papers and comment upon them or post them on a bulletin board for the class to share.

A totally different type of school writing program is a "writer's workshop." Children write daily or several times a week. They must decide on topics, write drafts, and help each other make revisions by conferring with each other.

It can be difficult for children to become fluent when they spend little time practicing writing. That is one reason you need to provide time for writing at home. Children who are always assigned topics for writing never learn how to find something to write about or to discover how an audience reacts to something they have written. Home writing can expand the kinds of writing children do. Children need to write factual reports, letters, persuasive pieces, and stories. They need to write for a variety of audiences as well.

Reading educators spend a lot of time talking about the importance of developing the reading habit. Writing habits are equally important to acquire and maintain. They cannot be acquired if a child is writing only once a week. Your goal can be for your child to write daily.

Much of school writing that is compressed into half hour slots of time is "hurry-up writing." The goal is to finish fast and not necessarily produce high-quality work. You can compensate for that undesirable by-product of school scheduling. Your child needs to be able to work on a piece over a longer period of time and to revise that piece until he is satisfied that it is of high quality. Your young writer discovers that if he starts a story and then returns to it for several days, he brings fresh insights to his writing each time and his story will be a better one in the end.

You should become actively involved in advocating daily school writing periods that last longer than half an hour. The way to acquire that additional time for writing is to cut back on the language arts, spelling, and handwriting textbook time and to use the revision process as a way of providing necessary instruction in those basic skills.

Informal Writing

Informal writing is like daily practice. It's like piano exercises or drills for a sport. When your child writes, these exercises are camouflaged. He is writing for other purposes, but practice is a natural outcome. Your child doesn't need formal drill such as copying sentences over several times. Instead, repetition naturally occurs and becomes his drill. His messages become repetitious "I love you's." His stories all begin the same way. His homemade Valentines are virtually duplicates of each other. Repetition then, serves a useful function. The goal of informal writing is quantity, not necessarily quality (as in formal writing). The more your child writes, the more practice he gets.

The one type of writing that is truly informal is diary writing. At one point or another, practically all children begin diaries. Usually it is the example of others that gets them started—Ann Frank's diary, the Laura Ingalls Wilder stories, or the diary of a relative or friend. You might want to take your child to museums that have diaries; he might be interested in logs kept by adventurers such as the pioneers or astronauts. The library is a good place to hunt out diaries. And after reading the diaries of others, your child may want to begin his own.

Illustration 54 contains excerpts from a child's first diary. Her teacher had asked her to keep one during the week she missed school due to a family trip. The child became fascinated with making entries after each event.

A trip or stay at summer camp offers a good opportunity for starting a diary. Your child might enjoy sharing his diary of camp experiences. You might keep letters you've exchanged as a diary. Or, your child might like to keep his diary private. You need to honor that request.

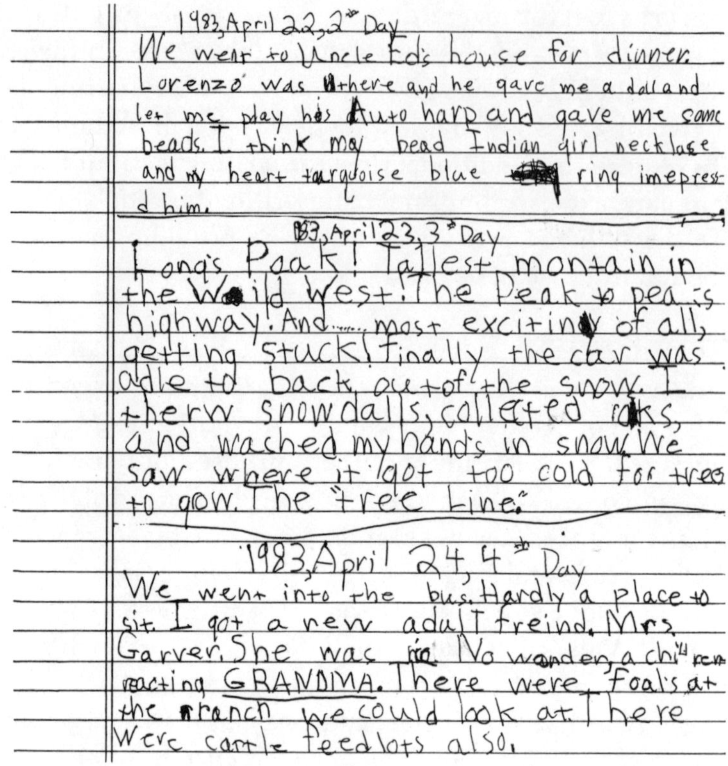

1983, April 22, 2ᵈ Day

We went to Uncle Ed's house for dinner.
Lorenzo' was there and he gave me a doll and
let me play his Auto harp and gave me some
beads. I think may bead Indian girl necklase
and my heart turquoise blue ✖ ring imepress-
d him.

83, April 23, 3ᵈ Day

Long's Peak! Tallest montain in
the Wild West! The Peak ✖ pea is
highway! And..... most exciting of all,
getting stuck! finally the car was
able to back out of the snow. I
therw snowdalls, collefed rocks,
and wached my hands in snow. We
saw where it got too cold for tree
to gow. The "tree Line."

1983, April 24, 4ᵗʰ Day

We went into the bus. Hardly a place to
sit. I got a new adulT freind. Mrs.
Garver. She was ✖. No wonder, a chil rem
reacting GRANDMA. There were foal's at
the ranch we could look at. There
Were cattle feedlots also.

Illustration 54

Diaries may focus on one topic: an athletic experience, a
musical experience, a first play. Or, they may be multi-topical
when children write about anything that's on their minds. One
child kept a diary of the family's experiences at their summer
cabin in Maine. Another began a diary of the life of a baby in the
family. One can imagine the fun that baby will have reading
about his adventures when he is older! We are all curious about
our beginnings, but to see your beginnings through the eyes of
an older brother or sister would be particularly intriguing.

A second type of informal communication is personal letter
writing. Only if personal letters are written regularly, however,
do they provide much practice at writing. Personal letters can be
a good rehearsal for stories written formally later on. The
excerpt from a child's letter to a friend in illustration 55 tells all
about her adventures in a storm. She could easily write a story

> We are having funny weather here, too.
> A couple of days ago there was a huge storm.
> I went to my Group Piano Lesson
> and it was so cozy that we decided
> to turn off the light and have
> candlelight. Jamie came late
> and reported a garbage can
> rolling down the street.
> She had thought it was
>
> a terrible thing, but then she recognized
> it as the neighbors' garbage can. Later
> I went home, and went out under my parasol
> to find David, the neighbors' cat. We bring
> him in a lot of times and feed him and
> hug him and he licks my ear so hard that
> it hurts. Finally I found him dripping under
> the eaves. I brought him into my room
> and rubbed and rubbed and rubbed him with
> my doll blanket until he was fairly dry. Then
> I let him out to climb between Daddy
> and the newspaper, knock over a lamp,
> gobble up all of Tosh's (Tosh is our own cat)
> food and lie down on my tummy to purr
> his happiness.

Illustration 55

about the storm using this letter as a base.

Children who write letters regularly practice the three components of the writing process. First, they rehearse what they are going to say in their letters. After something happens, they might say, "I think I'll tell Grandpa about that." Or, they think as they are getting up one morning, "Now what should I tell Aunt Jenny about when I write to her?" Then they compose and revise what they write, though they would not often rewrite a personal letter.

When your child becomes a fluent writer it is important for him to do some writing that does not have to be formally revised. Informal writing allows him to write his communications and send them as they are. While they should be proofread, personal letters can be mailed if they are not refined, for by their very nature, personal letters are unrefined writing.

There are two ways to get letter writing to be a part of your weekly routine. One is to write to a particular family member once a week, whether or not there is a reply in the interim. One child sets aside Saturday morning as the time to write to her grandparents. There is no doubt that the grandparents greatly enjoy this weekly communication for they always respond to it. But the child writes whether or not she has received the response by Saturday morning.

Another way to insure frequent writing is to have several regular correspondents: perhaps an aunt, uncle, or other family member; a friend who has moved away or one whom the child has met at camp. If your child keeps the letters he receives in a special place, when the weekly writing time arrives he can write to those from whom he has received letters during the week. Of course, other families might prefer more informal times for writing; each family has its own way of handling correspondence.

With telephones as popular as they are today, it is unfortunate that many families no longer correspond in writing. Letters can be kept, treasured, reread, and responded to thoughtfully, whereas phone calls require immediate and not always well-reasoned responses. Letters give, but do not *demand;* they say, "I was thinking of you. Respond when you have time!" Telephones can be intrusive! Both are wonderful ways to communicate, but it is sad when the phone replaces the personal letter for all of a family's communications.

Informal writing, then, gives your child opportunities to practice by writing on a regular basis. It allows him to complete some writing projects with a first draft, without revising each piece. Informal writing is not criticized and is enjoyed by its audience. It helps tie families and friends more closely together. One of the many values of informal writing is the fact that it makes formal writing easier and better.

Formal Writing

Formal writing is for a more public audience. The audience might be your child's peers, teachers, parents, relatives, or friends, or he may be writing for a contest, a neighborhood newspaper, or a magazine. Formal writing, by its very nature, is more refined than informal writing. It makes writers vulnerable because it receives criticism. For this reason, formal writing and informal writing need to be balanced in children's experience. Children who write only in school (and school writing in almost all cases is formal writing) rarely become enthusiastic writers because everything they write is judged. Informal writing is more relaxed and probably contributes more to the writing habit than formal writing does.

There are many, many forms of formal writing, but each progresses through three stages in its preparation. The first stage of formal writing is prewriting. The more time a child spends in prewriting, or planning, the easier the second, or composing stage will be. The third stage is revision. Not all formal writing is revised to the same degree, but if it is to be shared with an audience, the writing probably does need some revision.

Some types of formal writing are stories, essays, and reports typical of science and social studies classes, editorials and persuasive writing, directions, how-to articles, poetry, and news reports. Because there is such a wide variety of formal writing, many aspects of it can be encouraged at home. In one neighborhood, for example, the children produce a neighborhood newspaper. There is a great deal of interviewing, prewriting, writing, and revision which includes editing done by the children themselves. They sell advertisements, run a lost-and-found station, collect jokes from neighbors, publish neighborhood news, tell of sporting events that neighborhood children participate in, share neighborhood news, and print the best stories of the children on the block. Similar child-initiated efforts have resulted in nationally distributed publications of children's writings. *Stone Soup, The McGuffey Writer,* and *Wombat* are magazines totally devoted to the publication of works by and for children.

Most magazines publish children's works along with the writings of adults. Examples are listed in Appendix C. Writing for formal publication can be especially rewarding, since children see their work in published form. A neighborhood publication is not hard to produce if you have access to ditto machines. Children can write and even illustrate their work on the dittos.

Photocopied publications are more expensive.

Your child can bind his own books or story collections and save them or give them as gifts. Some children's writings have actually been published as books (on the Rubik's Cube, for example). Most will never see the light of publication, but the discipline which accompanies the writing process will aid your child in many other ways. He should not compose pieces solely to enter contests or publish their results; the writing process itself needs to be valued.

Prewriting or Rehearsal

The first step in writing is prewriting. The more time and thought given to writing at this stage, the easier the next stage—composing—will be. The first thing your child has to do when writing a piece is to decide on a topic. Many writers claim that this is the most important and neglected step in the writing process. When you or your child's teacher tell him what to write, he may do two things. He may write something that he is not especially well prepared to write, or he will not think about topic selection.

Some topics evolve rather naturally. There has been a bad winter storm and a child wants to tell what happened. A child has just received a tool kit and wants to record what he has made with it. Or, there is a need for a manual that other children can follow. Other topics are harder to come by.

A good way to decide upon a topic is for your child to list all of the potential topics that he might write about. Then, your child can ask questions that will help in the decision. Questions might include:

Which topic do I know the most about?

Which topic is the most interesting to me?

Which topic would my audience be most interested in?

Which topic is the most timely?

In this manner, you discard some topics because they have no audience appeal or because they would require too much research in order to find enough information. But another topic, if it is not written at the moment, will no longer be of interest. Children write best about what they have experienced, what is important to them, and what they care about. The fantasy

Hillary wrote about in illustration 56 evolved naturally from her keen interest and involvement with Halloween.

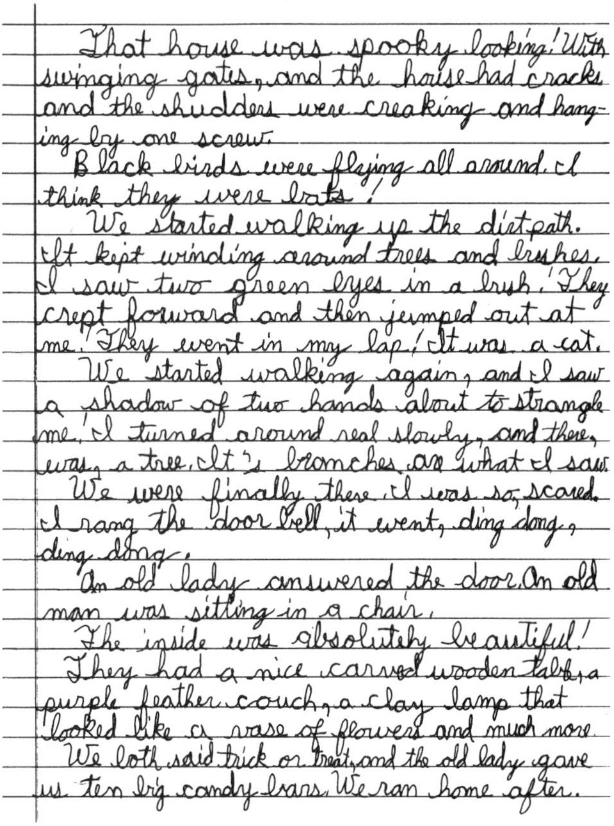

That house was spooky looking! With swinging gates, and the house had cracks and the shudders were creaking and hanging by one screw.
Black birds were flying all around. I think they were bats.
We started walking up the dirt path. It kept winding around trees and bushes. I saw two green eyes in a bush. They crept forward and then jumped out at me. They went in my lap. It was a cat.
We started walking again, and I saw a shadow of two hands about to strangle me. I turned around real slowly, and there was a tree. It's branches are what I saw.
We were finally there. I was so scared. I rang the door bell, it went, ding dong, ding dong.
An old lady answered the door. An old man was sitting in a chair.
The inside was absolutely beautiful! They had a nice carved wooden table, a purple feather couch, a clay lamp that looked like a vase of flowers and much more.
We both said trick or treat, and the old lady gave us ten big candy bars. We ran home after.

Illustration 56

Once the topic is selected, it is best to think about it for a time before putting pencil to paper. The second stage of prewriting is often called the rehearsal stage because the writer is thinking about what might be said in the piece. Usually, he needs to narrow down the topic. Children used to be taught to outline their writing. They often wrote their pieces, then developed the outline within them if both were requested by a teacher. While outlining may be helpful in some cases, a rigid outline often limits the spontaneity of the writing or prohibits the smooth flow of thoughts from one idea to another.

Rehearsal is a more informal outline. One teacher uses a system called the sunshine approach. Each of his fourth graders

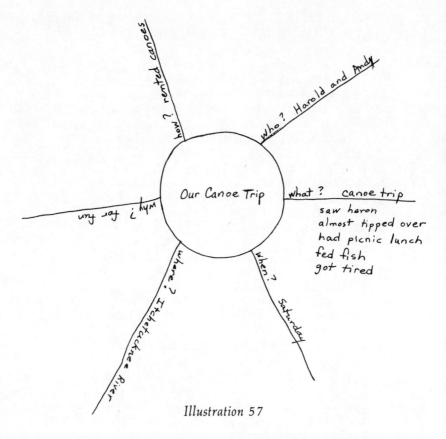

Illustration 57

draws a circle for the sun and then writes a topic inside it, as in illustration 57. Then, they make rays for their suns, affixing subtopics on them—the who, what, when, where, why, and how of their stories.

Some writings lend themselves to making lists of topics to be included. Personal and business letters fall into this category. One child regularly makes lists of points to remember when she is writing to her granny, as in illustration 58.

Sometimes you can't outline ahead of time. The story flows as the child is writing. For young children, drawing a picture provides the rehearsal. One child, when asked what he was going to write about replied, "I don't know. I haven't drawn my picture yet." It is best not to force your child to outline his writing but to observe what forms rehearsal naturally takes.

A child can rehearse mentally, or he may want to talk with others about the topic and see what ideas they have for the

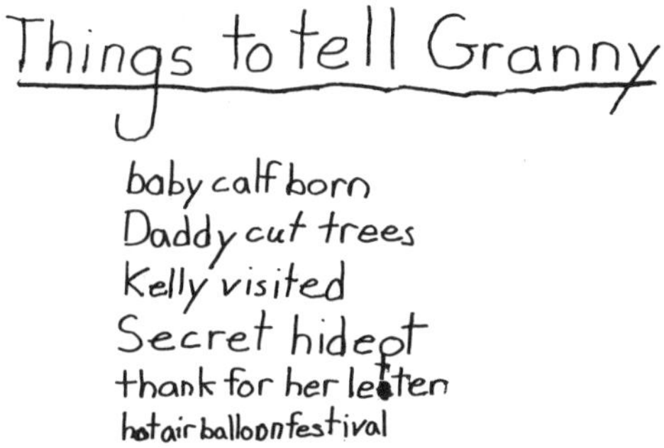

Things to tell Granny

baby calf born
Daddy cut trees
Kelly visited
Secret hideot
thank for her letter
hotair balloon festival

Illustration 58

content. Some authors claim that they really wrote their works while commuting in their car, rehearsing what they were going to say, so that when they came to actually putting it into writing, the text just flowed. That is the ideal writing situation. Ironically, it is often the most neglected aspect of writing done in school. In school, teachers are often constrained by limited time slots, so they place a deadline when children must finish. In their rush to meet the deadline, children do not give adequate thought to their topic selection and to how they are going to write their piece before rushing to get some words on the paper.

A third aspect of prewriting is accumulating information. While some writings are totally creative and do not include the collection of data, most are better if the child has researched the topic prior to writing about it. Your child can list all possible sources of information on the topic—magazines, books, live interviews, and observations. Children rarely use the last two sources and they are often the best sources. If your child is writing about new cars, for example, instead of relying solely on published literature for information, an interview with a new car salesperson would provide a different perspective. Your child should constantly be on the lookout for different perspectives on his topics. A mechanic has a different perspective than a salesperson, who in turn has a different perspective than an individual who is purchasing a car. Direct experience is the best source of information on a topic. The ideal time to write about new cars is when your child has lived through the experience of either riding in one or having the family purchase one. The ideal time to write about dolphins getting beached is after seeing it happen. Your child can use his direct experiences to generate topics to write about and to find information about a topic. When your child writes from his own experiences, he can better defend what he has written. His writing is apt to be clearer, more believable, and better documented. That is why writing personal letters or diaries about his experiences is a good preparation for writing in more formal ways on those same topics.

One of the most important skills you can help your child develop is notetaking. Families sometimes have encyclopedias and other reference books which children use as sources of information for school reports. The tendency of young children is to copy whatever information they want. You can teach your child to take brief notes by supplying him with notecards or adding machine tape. After he has written notes on the tape, he can cut it into pieces. The separate pieces or cards, grouped by topic, are now clearly organized by paragraph for writing.

Composing

The actual composing process involves getting the ideas into writing. Again, in most school situations under the pressure of time, children just sit down and write. Experienced authors rarely do this, for they know that to just sit down and write makes the writing more difficult. What do experienced authors do? What do you do when you are about to write? You make something hot to drink. You sharpen every pencil in the house (even though you write at a typewriter). You get a snack from the fridge. And then you sit down and write a few words! Then you go check the mail and perhaps pay a bill. Finally you go back to writing. It is not until after several preliminary starts that the writing generally flows. But when it comes out, it is of high quality.

Your child is rarely allowed the same luxury as a writer. He is asked to write quickly. No wonder he rushes the process and creates lower quality products. Most children, even after they are fluent writers, write at a leisurely pace. They stop periodically to read what they have written and then add to it. Sometimes they share their writing in progress with a receptive audience. At that point they stop and read the selection aloud to get feedback. Composing and revision are often cyclical with children—they write, get advice, revise, then write some more, share it, and then revise.

Most children talk while they are writing. Even after they are fluent they may hum, sing, or read aloud what they have written to themselves. Writing is not a quiet activity. Nor is it a solitary activity, as it might be for adults.

Children are not allowed the luxury of concentrating upon their work the way experienced writers do. In school, there are constant, unavoidable interruptions. At home, parents interrupt their children unnecessarily, yet object when their children do the same. Writers should be given uninterrupted time, for once there is an interruption, it can take considerable time to get back on task.

Mature writers throw out far more of their writing than they ever complete, yet we rarely allow children the luxury of throwing away their writings. Only a few of your child's pieces will be refined for distribution to outside audiences. The rest are not good enough, and your child needs to learn to discriminate between those that are suitable for revision and those that are not.

Children compose differently when they realize that revision is a part of the composing process. It is interesting to see the change in a child's paper when this light dawns. For example, Janelle thought that her first draft would be the final one. Her handwriting was carefully controlled, and there were few erasures. When she learned that this would be a first draft, her handwriting became sloppy and there were erasures and scribbles all over the place. The contents flowed more easily and, in the long run, it was a better piece.

When your child is composing, he needs scrap paper which should be different from the final paper. And he needs a wastepaper basket. It is helpful if you are around in case he wants to read his pieces aloud to get some feedback, either during composing or after the piece is written.

Revision

The final step in the composing process is revision. Professional authors revise for many drafts, often as many as twenty before their works are published. If professionals need this much revision, what about children who are just learning to write? We undervalue writing when we accept children's first drafts as the best they can do. Again, in school there are time restraints and children not only have little time for revision, they are graded on their first drafts.

The first step in revising a piece is to read it aloud to a sympathetic, if somewhat critical, audience. The following questions should be answered to the author's satisfaction:

• Did my audience get the main idea? Ask them to tell in one sentence what the piece is about. If they can't, or if their sentence does not match your intention, revision is necessary.

• Does the written piece say what I thought it did? Ask the audience to recall everything they can about your story. Here you find out what is missing, or what did not communicate as it was intended.

• Did I leave anything out? As the audience asks questions you may think, "But I already said that." If there is still a question in the audience's mind, revision is necessary.

• What else is needed? Have the audience tell what else could be added to the piece. What other questions do they have about the topic?

• What is not needed? Have the audience tell what parts of the piece did not add to the story.

When your child first revises his work, he needs to write as much as he can on a topic. His feedback will consist mainly of things to add. Later, with some types of writing, he'll have to delete words or move them around by cutting and pasting or using arrows. It is harder to refine by deletion than by addition, but getting rid of superfluous and extraneous information is an essential part of the writing process.

There are two ways that you can help your child get started on revising his writings. After he has written a rough draft, have him read it to you and ask him questions about it. His responses to the questions he wants to answer can be added to the bottom of the piece with tape if no space is available. Illustration 59 shows an example. Pam had written about her dog when he was a puppy. A friend asked what else he did and Pam tacked her response on to the end of the story.

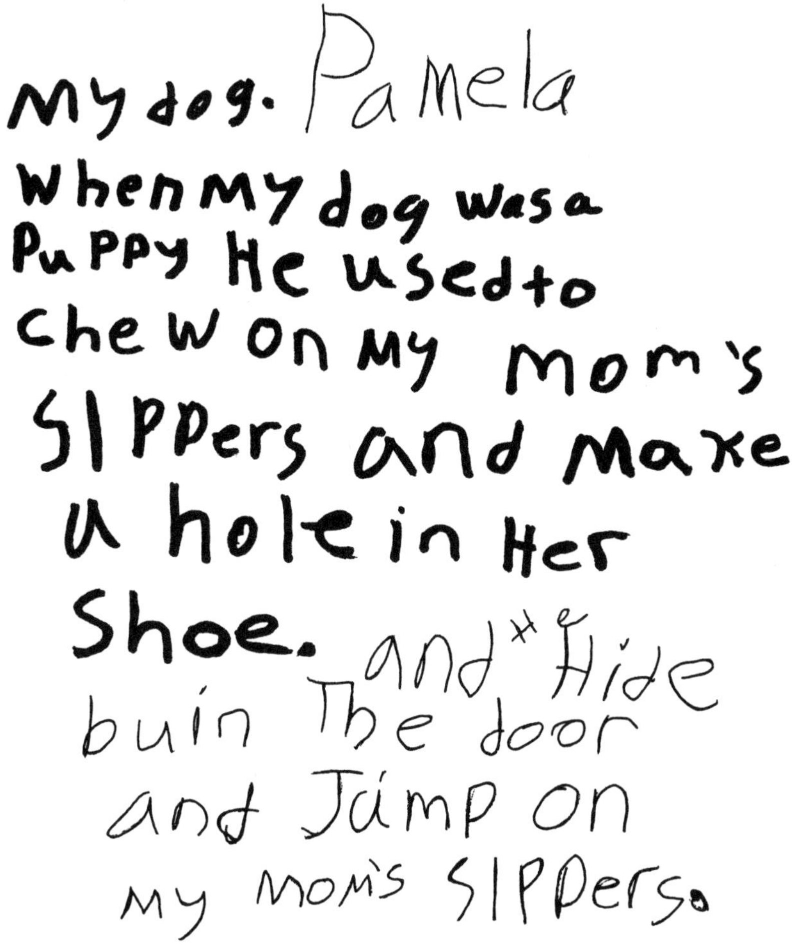

My dog. Pamela

When my dog was a Puppy He used to chew on my mom's Slppers and make a hole in her Shoe. and Hide buin The door and Jump on my mom's Slppers.

Illustration 59

It is important that when you ask questions you refrain from offering advice. If you say, why don't you tell what happened when the dog got lost, and the child does alter his story to do that, it is no longer totally his story, it is partly yours as well. But if you ask, "What happened when the dog got lost," your child can decide whether or not to answer that question, and the authorship of the piece is still his.

Another way to help your child learn how to revise is to act as his secretary. As he reads his piece to you, he can tell you what he would like to change and you can make the alterations on his first draft, as in illustration 60 a, so that all he has to do is

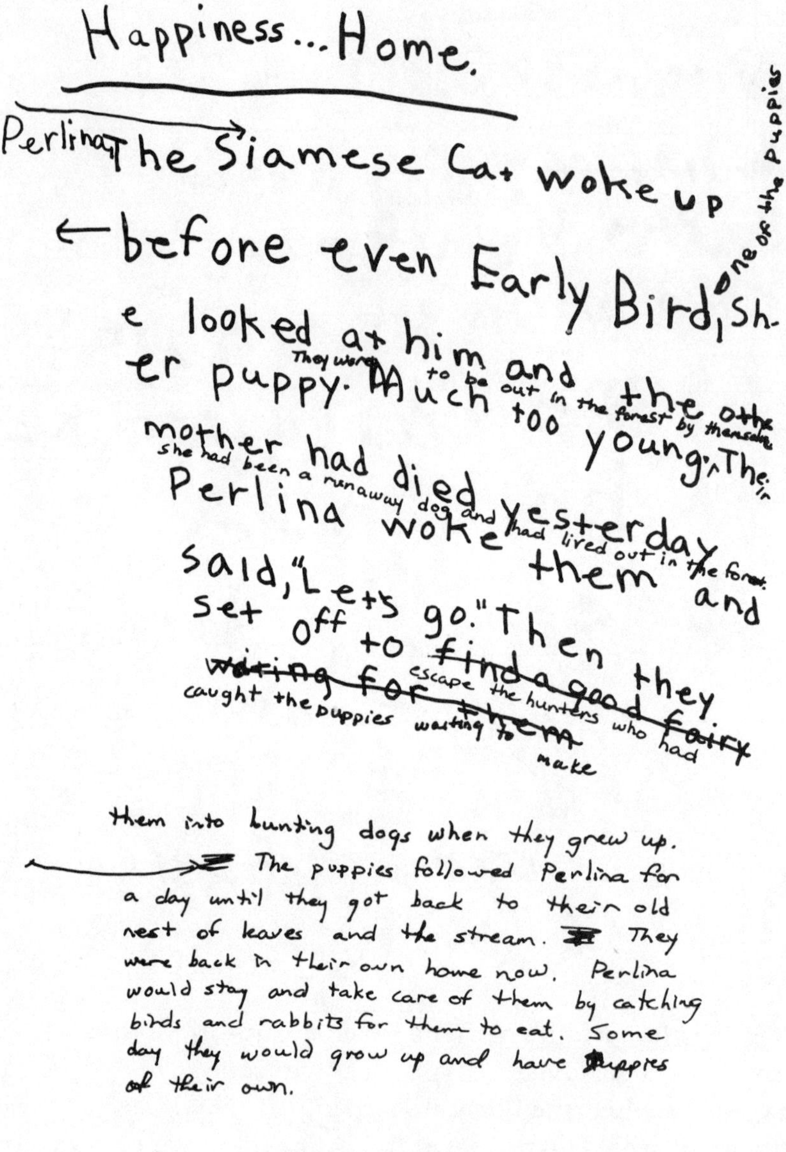

Happiness...Home.

Perlina The Siamese Cat woke up *One of the puppies*

← before even Early Bird. Sh-
e looked at him and the other puppy. Much too young. The
They were to be out in the forest by themselves
mother had died yesterday.
she had been a runaway dog and had lived out in the forest
Perlina woke them and
said, "Let's go." Then they
set off to ~~find a good fairy~~
~~waiting for them~~
escape the hunters who had
caught the puppies waiting to make

them into hunting dogs when they grew up.
The puppies followed Perlina for
a day until they got back to their old
nest of leaves and the stream. They
were back in their own home now. Perlina
would stay and take care of them by catching
birds and rabbits for them to eat. Some
day they would grow up and have puppies
of their own.

Illustration 60 a

to copy it over. An example of a child's revision is in illustration
60 b. Again, it is important not to give advice but merely write
down your child's suggestions for revision. It is not your story
but his, and he will feel a lot better about writing if you don't
shake his confidence by offering suggestions.

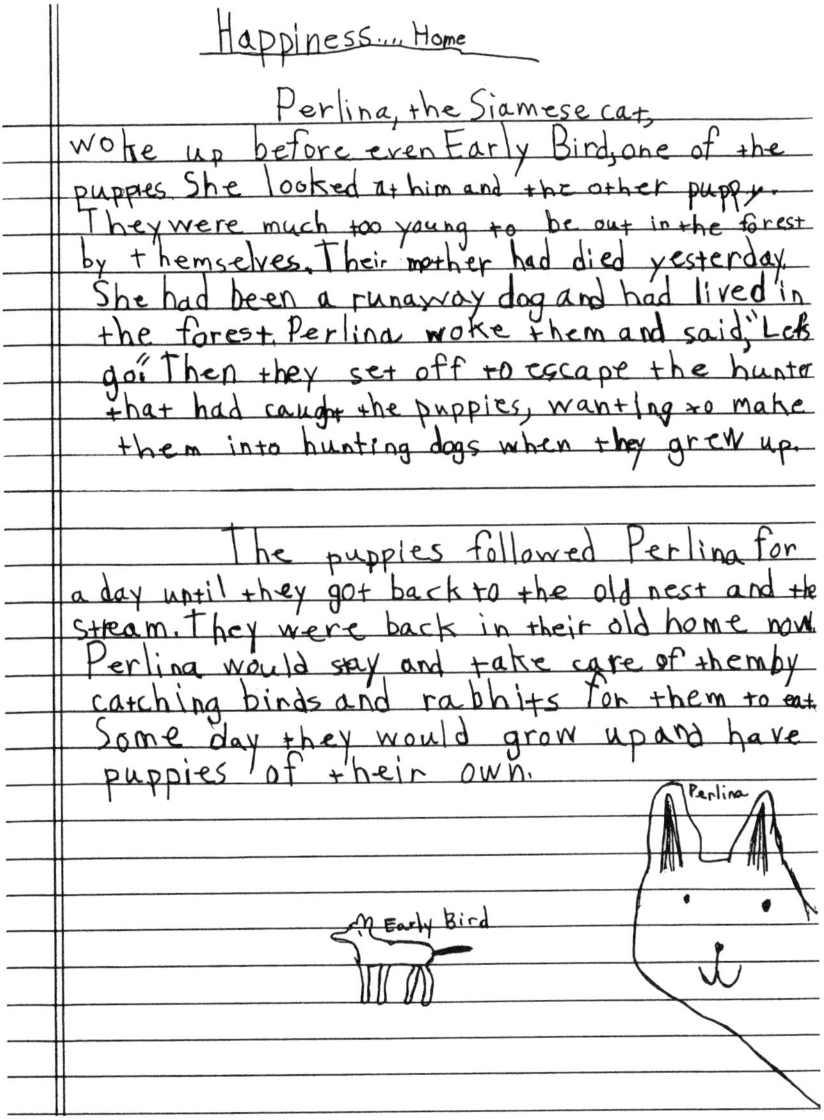

<u>Happiness.... Home</u>

Perlina, the Siamese cat, woke up before even Early Bird, one of the puppies. She looked at him and the other puppy. They were much too young to be out in the forest by themselves. Their mother had died yesterday. She had been a runaway dog and had lived in the forest. Perlina woke them and said,"Let's go." Then they set off to escape the hunter that had caught the puppies, wanting to make them into hunting dogs when they grew up.

The puppies followed Perlina for a day until they got back to the old nest and the stream. They were back in their old home now. Perlina would stay and take care of them by catching birds and rabbits for them to eat. Some day they would grow up and have puppies of their own.

Perlina

Early Bird

Illustration 60 b

The second part of the revision process, once the content is refined, is to proofread the piece for mechanical and spelling refinement. As your child is reading aloud, some need for changes in punctuation and spelling may appear.

If your child's written work is only to be shared orally, you can omit this step in the revision process, but if the piece is to be shared in written form, your child needs to correct it. Reading the piece out loud to a friend or to you provides an opportunity for mutual editing of the piece. You can make proofreading into a small game by putting a mark in the margin of each line where there is an error. Then your child can see if he can find and correct the errors. At this stage, your help *is* needed. All of the ideas in the paper are his; you are merely helping him proofread so others can read his ideas.

For this final proofreading, it is helpful for your child to have a "rules" book of some sort and a children's dictionary.

Don't underestimate the value of revision. We have a quantity-over-quality society. In school, children are encouraged to "get things done," not to do the very best job possible. One notices, for example, when one visits England that the quality of writing displayed in the schools is very much higher than the quality of writing in American schools. Each piece is carefully written and revised a number of times. The final piece is a work of art (often decorated in the margins and illustrated). Our children tend to rush to get things done, and in doing so, they fail to really stretch their writing ability.

In "The Doll House," in illustration 61 a, Ellen wrote the questions Dimitri asked in the margins and then attended to them in her revision. She added a concluding sentence to make the observation of clashing colors have a resolution. In her revision in illustration 61 b, Ellen added colorful words, like "clashed" instead of "looked bad" and "grew" instead of "get".

It is obvious that good writing does not occur in one sitting. Your child needs to return to his pieces over and over again. Keeping the earlier drafts helps your child see the progress he has made and helps him value the revision process. Two folders are needed—one for work in progress and one for work completed. Periodically, your child can go through his completed works, read them, and discard those that he does not wish to keep permanently. Making these decisions helps him discriminate among his writings, finding those of higher quality and determining what makes one piece better than another.

Computers may revolutionize the revision process for children. The Bank Street College has developed a very simple word-processing program called the Bank Street Writer which

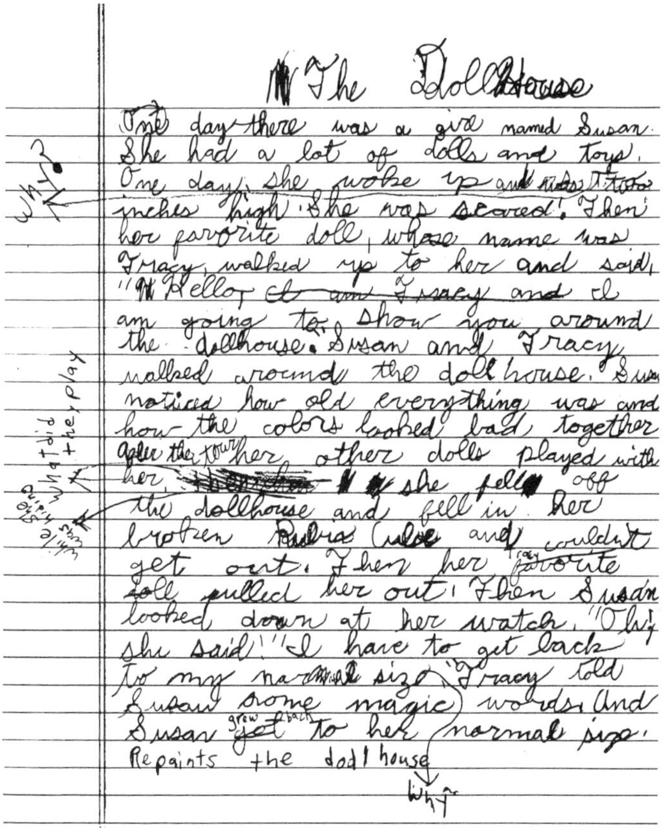

Illustration 61 a

is compatible with the Apple, Atari, and Commodore computers. Children who use the Bank Street Writer may find revision so simple that they eagerly revise their writing, but it takes children time to adjust to using the standard word processor. They don't automatically use all of the technology it contains. Early testing found that children who typically wrote one-and two-page stories churned out five pages or more with the Bank Street Writer. Children who had been reluctant to write at all were clamoring for time at the machine. The Bank Street Writer is available through computer stores and mail order firms.

Reading, Writing, and Thinking

Everyone knows that reading has a powerful impact on writing. Children's early stories are often retellings of familiar tales.

The Doll House

One day there was a girl named Susan. Susan had a lot of dolls and toys. One day, Susan woke up and was only two inches high, because accidentally before bed she had swallowed some shrinking pills. She was so scared when she woke up! Then her favorite doll, whose name was Tracy, walked up to Susan and said," Hello, I am going to show you around the doll house". Susan and Tracy walked around the doll house. Susan noticed how old everything was and how the colors clashed. After the tour, Susan played hide-and-go-seek with her other dolls. As she was hiding she fell into her broken Rubix Cube and couldn't get out of it. Tracy pulled her out. Then Susan looked down at her watch and cried "Oh, I have to get back to my normal size so I can eat lunch". Tracy told Susan some magic words and Susan grew back to her normal size. The next day Susan repainted the doll house.

By Ellen Berg

Illustration 61 b

Children learn to alter story lines and gradually use their literature background for their own stories. What people don't know is that writing has a powerful influence on reading, as well.

As children write they use advanced reading-comprehension techniques while making decisions about their writing. One of the key reading-comprehension skills is recognizing the main idea. Starting with topic selection, through the composing process, and in revision, the writer is constantly asking, "Am I getting my message across?" Writers acquire much deeper sensitivity to the main idea than readers generally do. Mature writers also know that the introduction to a piece must captivate their audience or else whatever follows it will never be read. This leads them to recognize the importance of opening sentences in the published writing they read. As your child constructs a story, he can use techniques much like those of professional writers to develop a plot. Writing makes these techniques more obvious to the reader.

Another reading-comprehension skill is remembering the sequence of events in a selection. As your child develops plots, he learns the importance of a logical sequence of events. Story retelling helps children develop reading comprehension skills. Since young writers often use stories they have read as models for stories they are writing, reading enhances writing, which, in turn, improves reading comprehension.

Finding details is another reading-comprehension skill which writing enhances. As your child is encouraged to give details in his own writing, he becomes alert to details in the writing of others. The revision process in writing is particularly helpful in developing analytical skills.

Synthesis is another high-order thinking skill used in reading comprehension, to generalize about what has been read or to draw conclusions. Your child writer must draw conclusions so well in writing that the reader can comprehend the logic behind them.

Finally, prediction is a reading-thinking skill greatly enhanced by writing. A good reader is constantly anticipating what will happen next in the story. One child, having read all but the last chapter of *The Black Stallion,* not only predicted a number of different endings to the story but also ranked them in the order in which he hoped they would occur. Writing helps your child develop a "sense of story" which greatly facilitates his reading comprehension.

Writing makes a person think in ways that he does not have to while reading. It requires analysis of the ways words and passages are built.

Writers are inevitably readers, but the reverse is not always true. It would seem, then, that one way to help children become better readers and thinkers is to help them become more active writers.

Chapter 6

Handwriting

"How do you make an 'R'?"
"Please **teach me cursive!"**
"But I *can't* **read it. It's in cursive!"**

Unless children develop the ability to write legibly and with some speed, they will never become enthusiastic writers. Two essentials—the ability to manipulate writing tools and an appreciative audience for the finished product—are crucial to the development of handwriting. The growth of this skill begins with handwriting awareness, progresses through handwriting readiness, to writing in manuscript and then in cursive.

Handwriting Awareness

Long before they can write alphabet letters, young children do a lot of thinking about handwriting. Studies show that toddlers often scribble with intent, differentiating between their pictures and their "writing." This "handwriting awareness" precedes actual handwriting development and helps place the skill in a framework which makes more sense to young children.

Older children make finer distinctions, such as noticing different types of writing. Even after they have been taught they continue to write some letters like those in typed texts (typically the **t** and the **a**), rather than in the correct manuscript forms, as in illustration 62. They experiment with and manipulate alphabet letters into various deviations of their forms. Circles appear over i's. Children discover the boundaries of readability by finding how far they can deviate from the standard form and still have their handwriting be legible. This play with writing develops handwriting awareness, which is

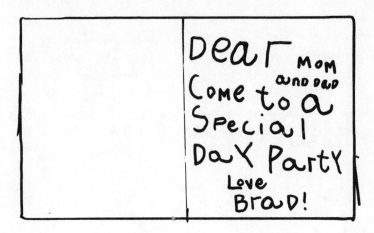

Illustration 62

needed as actual handwriting skill develops.

Children are very sensitive to writing. One young child noticed that her babysitter was writing in cursive, "so she must have had something important to write." Obviously, to this child, adults use cursive in their "important" writing, something which children are eager to emulate. The impact of such close observation of adult writing is evident in the ease with which young children teach themselves to write their names in cursive.

It is helpful, then, to expose your child to writing in natural ways, not just so he will learn it has meaning but so he will learn to think about how alphabet letters are formed. Then, when he develops handwriting skill, the process is easier for him to understand and duplicate.

Three encounters with writing are especially important. The first is the opportunity to observe adults in the process of writing to see how alphabet letters and words are actually formed.

A second avenue for developing handwriting awareness is play with writing. As young children trace and color in alphabet letters, as they make letters into designs and vice versa, as they cut writing out of magazines and newspapers, and as they play with various forms of writing, they are acquiring a vast storehouse of knowledge.

The third encounter that builds handwriting awareness is

Illustration 63

Illustration 64

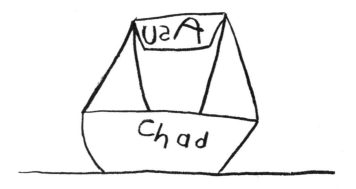

Illustration 65

environmental print. Advertising logos often appear in children's early drawings. "E.T." appears often on early writings. Had Chad watched the America's Cup Races when he drew his ship bearing a flag from the USA (in illustration 65)? The printed reading materials in children's environments, then, is influential in developing handwriting awareness.

Handwriting Readiness

Young children develop handwriting readiness by drawing, scribbling, and writing. These paper and pencil activities are essential, but many other activities can aid in the development of handwriting skills as well. There are essentially five prerequisite skills involved in the development of handwriting: small muscle coordination, eye-hand coordination, manipulation of tools, mastery of basic strokes, and letter perception.

Small muscle coordination is the ability to control the small muscles of the hand. These muscles need to develop before your child can manage a writing tool. The best exercises to develop small muscles are molding and manipulating activities. Modeling clay, Play Doh, and real dough help children develop their small hand and finger muscles. Playing with doll house furniture, garages and cars, Legos, Tinker Toys, and puzzles also strengthens these little muscles.

Children who don't hold their writing tool correctly, who are slow writers, or whose work appears sloppy or uncontrolled, benefit from these muscle-strengthening activities.

Eye-hand coordination is the process whereby your child's fingers obey the message transmitted by his brain. Some precision work activities which promote eye-hand coordination and also strengthen small muscles include piecing together Legos and Tinker Toys or balancing blocks.

Sewing is a more difficult eye-hand coordination activity. For your young child, you can start with a large darning needle and use yarn to sew through burlap. Use a wooden frame to hold the burlap until your child masters the up-and-down directionality of sewing. Stringing beads prepares children for sewing. Striking or hitting something, such as playing a drum or a triangle, hammering, or playing a piano, are activities that promote eye-hand coordination. Children who have difficulty writing on the lines, forming alphabet letters so that lines meet and circles close, or writing letters in uniform size, benefit from eye-hand coordination activities.

Manipulating a writing tool comes from practice with using utensils of any sort. Children who put holes in their paper, who write with clenched teeth, who get cramps, or who tire easily when writing, may not be holding the tool correctly. They benefit from more exposure to tools. A pencil or pen is a handwriting tool in the same way that a fork, spoon, and knife are eating tools and a paintbrush is a painting tool. At home, children enjoy gardening and cooking; in school, they may work at sand and water tables. You can modify these activities for home. Give your child things to play with in the bath tub or provide a basin for water play outdoors in good weather. Likewise, your child may enjoy spending hours in a sand box or at the beach with buckets and shovels. These activities can greatly improve a child's writing legibility, speed, and endurance by improving how he holds writing tools.

The basic strokes for handwriting are circles and lines. As your child plays with tools, especially those for drawing and painting, he refines these basic strokes. Many children learn how to write their names before they have mastered basic strokes. They can copy an adult model and learn to write their names before they are actually ready to write in general. Mastery of basic strokes is a clear indication that children are ready to write. Illustration 66 shows the writing and drawing of a child who has almost mastered basic strokes. You'll notice that the intersections of her lines are not quite perfect in both her drawing and her writing.

"Once upon a time there was a honey bear she wanted to borrow some honey so she asked the bees if she could and the bees said yes. The End."

When circles, straight lines, and slanted lines appear in your child's drawings of people, cars, trees, houses, and animals, and when the strokes are firm—starting where intended and stopping where intended, with crisp intersections—then handwriting is easy to learn. Its component parts have already been mastered. Children acquire the basic strokes through lots of

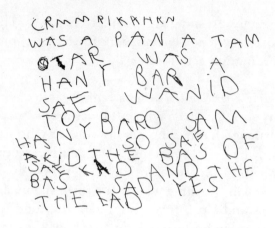

Illustration 66

drawing experience and through activities such as stirring and painting.

Letter perception is the ability to figure out how an alphabet letter is made. Your child needs exposure to writing, especially by observing an adult write and by being given the opportunity to play with writing. Letter perception includes those aspects of handwriting that make the manuscript letters readable: size, shape, slant, alignment, line quality, and spacing. It includes knowing how to form letters as well as what the letters should look like when they are completed.

Handwriting readiness, then, consists of five types of skills which children naturally acquire through their play experiences.

Don't underestimate the value of these play experiences, for they are vital. If your child begins writing without them, he will compensate for the skills he has not yet mastered and develop bad habits that will hinder his handwriting ability for the rest of his life.

Handwriting Tools

There are innumerable handwriting tools. Some are easier for beginners to use than others. The second chapter discusses the importance of supplying children with a variety of tools. In this section, we explore the impact these tools have on handwriting. Given their choice, young children usually select marker pens for writing. They prefer crayons for coloring, thick markers for large papers, and minimarkers for tiny scraps of drawing and writing paper. Children naturally select appropriate handwriting tools if given choices. What are the strengths and weaknesses of these tools?

Pencils, most commonly used for writing, are the most difficult tools to write with. Quite a bit of pressure is needed to make legible marks; their tips break, and they are not very colorful. Pencils should be longer than three inches and they should have good erasers. If your child is making holes in the paper while erasing, he needs sturdier paper or a tool that requires less pressure. Pencils are appropriate for children who are perfectionists and want everything to be correct, because with erasers they can make corrections easily.

Schools often use large primary pencils to teach handwriting, more often to save money than for any other reason. Their thicker leads do not break as easily as the thin ones found in number-two pencils. Some pencils have thinner diameters but contain the thicker lead. These thinner pencils are easier than the thicker ones for young children to grasp and control.

The best tool for beginning writers is the thin marker pen. It requires little pressure to make a firm, clear, and colorful mark on the paper. Minimarkers are enjoyable (and inexpensive) and match children's small hands. Markers, if they have been used previously for drawing, make a nice transition to writing.

Crayons are not as suitable for writing as are other tools, though they are perfect for coloring in pictures. You need to press hard to make bright marks with crayons. Their tips quickly become dull and they break rather easily.

Schools typically use thick crayons and thick marker pens for writing. Considering how hard it is to manipulate these tools with a proper grip, they are best left for drawing and coloring.

There are several gadgets that are useful for your child if he is not gripping the tool correctly. Plastic triangular grips which slip over the end of a writing tool can help children grasp the tool more easily. Pencils with molded handles provide a similar grip.

Writing tools should be held loosely. You should be able to slip the tool rather easily from the hand of your child as he is writing. To achieve this grip, have your child shake his hands, then gently balance the tool on the third finger, while using the thumb and first finger to steer it. Your child should keep his fingers off the shaved part of a pencil, about an inch away from the point of the tool. The pointer finger should be bent outward. If you have a preschool child, you should not push him to hold the tool correctly. He will, at first, draw and write holding his tool like a paintbrush. Gradually he will adjust and find a more comfortable position with which to control his strokes. At school age, the adjustment should be complete.

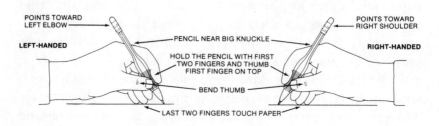

Illustration 67

Left-Handers

By the time children take a serious interest in learning to write, they typically have indicated a strong laterality or preference for either the left or the right hand. To determine your child's preferences, watch as he throws a ball, stirs sand in play, or eats. Place utensils directly in front of your child and see which hand he uses to pick things up and whether he switches from hand to hand. Generally, children adjust so that they are eating and drawing predominantly with one hand. Do not push your child to use the right hand, rather, allow him to select his own preference.

Left-handed children hold their writing tools in the same way that right-handed children do. It is helpful if they can watch left-handed adults write to develop handwriting awareness. Left-handers may write backwards more frequently than right-handers, especially if they are surrounded by right-handed writers. Left-handers should not crook their arms so that they can see the words they are writing because the writing smudges as their hand passes over it. If a left-hander develops a "crook," it is helpful to have him write on a chalkboard or other vertical surface. It is much more difficult to write with a "crooked" arm on the board. Left-handers should write exactly the way right-handers do, with the exception of their paper position.

How Handwriting Is Taught in Schools

Teachers usually teach children to form alphabet letters by first practicing basic handwriting strokes, often on lined paper, and then either tracing or copying letters in a workbook. Workbooks provide dotted or screened models for children to trace until they have mastered forming the alphabet letter; then they begin copying the letter.

It is vital that, as your child learns handwriting skills, he realizes that copying isn't writing and that alphabet letters, in isolation, convey no meaning. Children's concepts of writing should be advanced to the degree that children can distinguish between a word and an alphabet letter, and between writing and drawing before they are finally taught to form letters.

Sometimes, lined paper can be a problem for children who are just learning how to write. They might do better with unlined paper until their letters are uniform in size; then they have no problem staying on the lines. It is difficult for young children to concentrate on two things at once—staying on the lines *and* forming letters.

Tracing letters can hinder the development of basic strokes if children trace before they master the strokes. Sometimes in beginning writing instruction, teachers ask children to practice writing alphabet letters over and over again. This can become tedious and cause negative attitudes toward handwriting. As much as possible, children should practice handwriting when they are writing their own stories.

Some school programs just let children write and never systematically teach handwriting. You need to monitor your child's handwriting to be sure that he is not developing bad handwriting habits. If your child isn't getting instruction in handwriting at school, make sure he has real reasons to copy work over in polished handwriting at home.

The Order of Development in Handwriting

Just as composition development is evident from drawing and scribbling, technical skill at handwriting evolves from scribbling. The progression appears roughly as follows:

Progression of Handwriting Skills

1. Non-linear scribbles
2. Linear scribbles
3. Repeated designs
4. Mock letters
5. Random letters
6. Letters or numbers in a string
7. Letters or numbers clustered like words
8. Letters of inconsistent size over an inch tall
9. Letters of inconsistent size under an inch tall
10. Letters of uniform size/shape
11. Upper and lowercase letters used randomly
12. Letters of uniform size without reversals
13. Experiments with cursive writing
14. Upper and lowercase letters used correctly

While at all of the levels from 3 to 14, children play with writing. They color in letters, trace over letters, and turn letters into graphic designs. In illustration 68 Tameshra made a page of s's as she played while illustrating the page of a homemade book. Under the s's written by her mother, she tried her skill at making her own.

Learning How to Write

Children learn how to form alphabet letters both by playing

Illustration 68

with their own writing and by copying an adult model. It is important, then, for you to learn how to form the letters perfectly. Appendix A contains a sample of manuscript alphabet letters. The alphabet letters most often misformed by adults are the **e** (which is often rounded) and the **k** (which is made to look like an uppercase **K**). Often, people put upswings at the end of their manuscript letters similar to the way they would write cursive alphabet letters. These upswings make it harder for young children to learn to write. It is best for letters to be formed by sticks and circles.

When a child is having difficulty forming alphabet letters, it is tempting to write for him and have him trace your model. It's not a good idea for your child to trace or follow the dots for two reasons. First, when he traces, your child is concentrating on staying on the lines, not on developing letter perception or learning how the letter is formed. Tracing to form an alphabet letter is very different from the tracing that children do in play where they rarely stay on the lines. Tracing increases your child's dependency upon the model rather than helping him become independent.

Second, tracing inhibits the development of smooth, flowing, basic strokes. When tracing, children grit their teeth and slow their writing down to little tiny jerks rather than smooth flowing lines. When children play with writing, they are relaxed and are forming more flowing lines.

Tracing, then, is not advocated as a method of instruction, but when tracing occurs naturally in children's play with writing, you won't want to stop it. Try having your child copy instead of trace. If he asks how to form a particular alphabet letter or how to write a word, you can write the word on a piece of paper where he can copy it directly underneath your writing.

You'll want to get a copy of the alphabet used in your local school district so that your children won't have to change from one system of handwriting to another when they reach school age. Some schools use a form of italic handwriting and some start the children with cursive right from the beginning. Most schools have children begin with manuscript writing and then at the end of second grade or the beginning of third, introduce cursive. A cursive alphabet is found in Appendix B.

Manuscript writing needs to be of uniform size for letters that rise to half a space (**a, c, e, g, i, j, m, n, o, p, q, r, s, u, v, w, x, y,** and **z**) and for letters that are tall (**b, d, f, h, k, l,** and **t**, which is usually a bit shorter than the rest). Often adults write much smaller than children do, so when you write for your child, you need to try to write a bit larger than usual. One "mistake" children often make is to write letters which normally go below the line (**g, j, p, q,** and **y,**), above the line. You can help your child conceptualize the idea of writing on a line by drawing a line lightly before you write so that your "below-the-line letters" are seen as being below a line, as in illustration 69.

When should you give your child lined paper? In his efforts to be grown-up, he'll probably ask for writing paper with lines. But when he discovers how difficult it is to make his handwriting fit the lines, he'll discard lined paper.

When your child's alphabet letters are of uniform size, he can make the transition to lined paper rather easily, especially if the space between the lines is the same size as his letters. If there is any doubt about your child's readiness for lined paper, it is best to wait. Nothing is more frustrating for a writer than to master letter formation and then immediately have to think about the size of letters at the same time.

The child who wrote "The Special Horse" on unlined paper in illustration 70 is ready to make the transition to lined paper. Sometimes, teachers ask children to write on lined paper

Illustration 69

The special horse

Once upon a time there was
a flying horse. He was wild.
evreyome tried to catch
him. But they coulnd't. Well
atleast evreyone thout so.
But the king of that land had
a fine beeyootiful brave dauter.
One day she said I am going to
catch that horse. Nobody wanted
her to try but, A mystery
happend! When the horse saw
her coming she (The horses name was
Maude) just went up to Dahlia (That
was the princesses name) and nuzzuld her.
Dahlia took Maude home and took care
of her.

Dahlia

Maude

Illustration 70

with wider spaces than they have been used to. Most first-grade
children do write more legibly on the wide-lined paper. For some
children, however, this is actually a backward step. In that case,

try to substitute regular notebook paper for the wide-lined paper commonly used in early childhood grades. Some young children prefer to write smaller than the wide lines on first grade paper and do better if they can write naturally rather than make their writing larger.

When you write, use upper and lowercase letters as they would normally appear in written material. Children who learn all of their uppercase letters first must relearn them in lowercase once they get to school. Uppercase letters do not have to be larger than lowercase ones and are not, except in a few cases, easier to write. From the start, children can use uppercase and lowercase letters properly. Beginning writers will use the two intermittently. Uppercase **E**'s may be used because they are easier to write than the lowercase **e**'s (the same with **M,N,** and some other letters). Uppercase **B** and **D** are easier to differentiate than are their lowercase forms, which children often confuse, so they may prefer the uppercase versions. All of these adjustments come in time and should be ignored as children are just learning to write.

Making the Transition to Cursive Writing

Cursive writing has basic strokes that are slightly different from manuscript. Prior to making the transition, you can encourage your child to practice these basic strokes in designs and patterns as well as in his drawings. The basic strokes are the slant stroke, undercurve, downcurve, and overcurve.

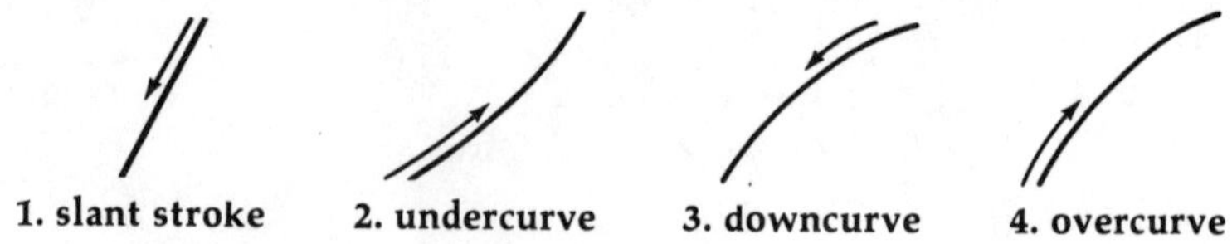

1. slant stroke 2. undercurve 3. downcurve 4. overcurve

Illustration 71

These strokes commonly appear in childrens' drawings of ocean waves, clouds, water, footballs, trees, and flowers. Your child needs to feel comfortable making these strokes just as he did making sticks and circles prior to learning manuscript writing.

Make sure your child can read in cursive before he learns to write in cursive. You'd never want to ask him to copy anything he can't read. One parent began writing lunchbox notes to her child in cursive in order to give him practice in reading it before he learned to write it.

Reversals

Many parents become concerned if their children form alphabet letters backwards or if they write in ways other than from left to right. Most of the time when children make reversals, they have not yet permanently learned the conventions of English writing. Chinese children write vertically; Americans write horizontally. A general awareness of this difference appears when children are still scribbling, but it takes a long time to master thoroughly top-to-bottom orientation and left-right directionality.

Actually, we form some alphabet letters with a first stroke that moves from right to left instead of from top to bottom or from left to right as most strokes go. These letters (**c, s, g,** and **j**) provide most of the reversal problems. Depending where children begin the letter, **N** can come out backward. Notice that Wendy wrote her alphabet perfectly except for the letters **J** and **S** in illustration 72.

Illustration 72

In illustration 73 Clyde made his J's backward on his picture of a jungle gym.

Children whose names are Samantha, Jack, Sam, or Natasha are more likely to write their names backward than children whose names are Danielle, Bob, or Amy.

Once a child writes the first letter backwards, it is not uncommon simply to continue to write the rest toward the left, giving a mirror image of the word. In illustration 74 Jonah

---

reversed his message because he reversed the first letter in his name and because he started writing at the right edge of the paper. He writes in the correct direction most of the time.

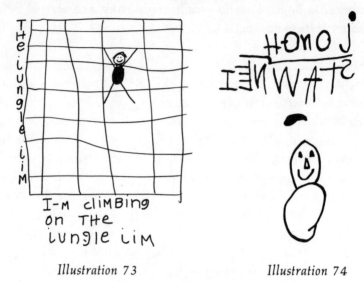

| Illustration 73 | Illustration 74 |

Starting at the right edge of the paper instead of the left contributes to reversal problems. Before they have learned to begin at the left, practically all children will start at the right and move toward the left. Also, when writing on lined paper, children often do not know what to do when they reach the end of a line. They may have begun at the left, but they have not yet learned the return sweep, so will return toward the left from the right (or go up or down).

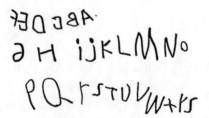

Illustration 75

In illustration 75, notice that when Joey began at the right, his letters (**A-G**) came out backwards. But when he writes from left to right, they are uniformly directionally correct.

Numerals provide special challenges to writing in a correct direction, as is shown in illustration 76. Children reverse the numbers 2, 3, 6, 7, and 9 long after they are writing most alphabet letters correctly. This may occur for several reasons. Children write numerals less frequently than they write words. Most alphabet letters open on the right (**c, e, f, k, r**), but a 3 opens on the left. The numerals 6 and 9 are easy to confuse.

Reversals in the preschool years are frequent and usually readily explainable from the child's developing concept of directionality and spacing. Only if reversals continue into the elementary grades and are accompanied by difficulty in learning to read are they really a problem. And, as has been mentioned earlier, left-handers are more prone to make reversals than are right-handers.

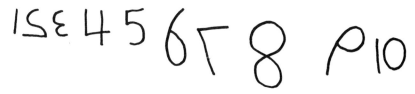

Illustration 76

If reversals persist long after your child is writing fluently, it is appropriate to have him trace the words which contain his letter reversals so that he gets the feel of the proper directionality. Teachers use sandpaper and other textured alphabet letters for this purpose.

Handwriting Problems

There are a number of fairly common problems which some children encounter as they learn to write. If you can determine the causes of those problems, you can solve them before your child develops negative attitudes toward writing.

Writing Slowly
If your child writes very slowly, it may be because he is holding the utensil too tightly. He needs to loosen his grip a bit. Some slow writers are perfectionists. They write slowly in order to

produce a perfect product. If your child is a perfectionist, give him scratch paper for rough copies so he can differentiate between writing that is polished and writing that is not. Other slow writers have never mastered the basic writing strokes. They carve each letter out carefully rather than using bold, basic strokes. These children benefit from more drawing, sketching, and doodling experiences which loosen up their muscles and allow them to develop their basic strokes.

Slow writers also may be holding their writing tools in an awkward, uncomfortable manner. Altering the hand position may cure that problem. If their writing is too large, give them smaller lined paper that helps reduce the size of their writing.

Children who can only write very slowly do not want to write. Writing takes too long and can be tedious work. Overemphasizing legibility can hinder speed, so balance and perspective are needed. Children write best when they are at a child-size table where their feet can touch the floor and they do not have to try to balance themselves and manipulate the writing tool at the same time. Children do not do their best writing when they write on a floor, bed, kitchen table, or stool.

Sloppy Handwriting

Sloppy writers are usually writing too fast. They rush to get their writing done so they can get on with something else. This is an attitude problem. Children who write only for school assignments don't see the need for good handwriting. They can get by with sloppy work. Sloppy writers need to revise their work for useful purposes, such as mailing it or putting it on display.

If your child writes sloppily, check to see if he is forming his letters correctly. Have him compare his writing to a standard model. Check to see if his handwriting has a uniform slant.

Sloppy handwriting can also result from sitting in an improper position without a clear, smooth, desk surface. Your child needs to have pride in his writing. Then he'll want his writing product to look nice.

Small Handwriting

Small writing can be a problem if it is hard to read. If you ask your child to write larger, and provide him with wider-spaced lined paper, the problem should be solved.

Incorrect Slant

Backhand slant is usually caused by the position of the paper on the desk. If you change the angle of the paper, the slant changes. You can tape your child's paper into the best position on the table until he gets used to the correct format.

Dysgraphia

Dysgraphia is a term applied to the rare child who, for some unexplainable reason, cannot write well at all. Manipulating the writing tool is inordinately difficult for this child, who otherwise can read and tell stories well. It is assumed that there is a brain dysfunction which prevents the child from being able to write. The dysgraphic child needs a lot of adult support and the opportunity to type whenever possible.

Maintaining Good Handwriting

There are two important goals of handwriting instruction: Children should write legibly and they should write with some speed. Children who write illegibly do not enjoy writing because they are unable to share their products with others.

Legible writing is often very closely related to attitudes at home. Some parents claim that there is no need for good handwriting because their children will end up using a typewriter or a word processor anyway, or they show little interest in their children's penmanship. Their children don't put forth the effort to produce a clear, legible form. On the other hand, other parents display and mail their children's writing. These children see a reason to work at perfecting handwriting.

Drill on isolated letters is meaningless and boring. Children can maintain good handwriting by writing often and for real communication. Sometimes children who are learning to write provide their own drill. One child, just learning to write her name in cursive, labeled every little box in her room with her name and its contents.

If you value your children's writing, keep folders of your children's best work, display their work, and write and mail letters, you'll have no trouble keeping your children's handwriting in good form. When children get sloppy in their handwriting, they can be shown the folder indicating their progress. Just as when children get sloppy with other habits, a simple reminder is often enough to turn the tide.

Typing and Word Processing

At very young ages, children enjoy playing with a typewriter or a word processor. They are fascinated with the way they can type an alphabet letter and have it appear on the screen or on the page in front of them. This kind of play with print requires less small muscle coordination than handwriting, so your child can enjoy it at an earlier age. Typewriter play does not allow your child to acquire letter perception as readily, however, because he cannot color in and trace over letters. It does give children greater awareness of alphabet letters and of their configurations in words. Play at a typewriter usually follows a progression of activity. First a child types at random. Then he systematically plays with alphabet letters and then with words. Older children make inventories of alphabet letters and numbers. They type out all of the words that they know.

A word processor offers one advantage that a typewriter does not have. It is more flexible. Children seem more willing to invent spellings on the computer for two reasons. First, they learn early on that with the word processor they can change what they type. There is usually a DELETE key which allows them to edit messages as they are typing. Secondly, because it is generally faster for young children to type than it is to write, children typically experiment more freely with type.

At these early stages children use the "hunt and peck" system for finding keys. This "hunt and peck" system aids their visual memory and greatly assists children in learning to recognize their alphabet letters. By the time children are composing fluently, however, you need to teach them to touch-type for, in the long run, "hunt and peck" typing is much slower than touch-typing. There are several software programs for computers which teach touch-typing in a game format. If children touch the correct keys, the computer performs, but if they don't, it doesn't. Schools offer touch-typing courses for children because many programs require that children be able to touch-type before they use a word processor. Touch-typing is necessary for computer programming as well. Many schools teach elementary school children how to write computer programs.

By the time they are in high school, children need to be able to type correctly and speedily in order to make maximum use of their writing talents. Some colleges require that all entering freshmen purchase small computers with word processing capabilities. Typed papers are routinely requested of high school and college students.

In addition to the Bank Street Writer, an inexpensive, user-friendly system for home computers, there are many word processing programs available. If you are interested in purchasing a word processor, you can try out several systems. Even minor differences in programs can be helpful or annoying, depending upon your individual needs and abilities.

Younger children today benefit more and more from their encounters with typewriters and word processors. Just as most homes now have television, in the very near future, they will also have computer systems with word processing capabilities. You need to be sure that your children become accomplished writers, both when they write in their own handwriting and when they type on a typewriter or word processor.

Chapter 7

Spelling

"I looked 'knee' up in the dictionary, but it's not under the N's!"
"Hey Mom, how do you spell 'gnome'?"
"You mean you can read MY spelling, too?"

Parents seldom realize the impact of their comments on children's writing. It is easy to recognize a child's mistakes, to point out a misspelled word or a comma used where a period should have been. Criticisms such as these focus the child's attention on the form of writing rather than on its function. Such criticisms can discourage young writers.

It is true that children need to learn how to spell and punctuate with precision, but the time to focus attention on these aspects of writing is **after** your child has become a fluent writer. Fluent writers can rather easily write anything they want to, though it may not be spelled or punctuated correctly. Prior to this, concentrate on the content of what your child writes and ignore the form. If the writing is illegible, ask your child to read the message to you. Then comment on what it says, not how it is written.

Spelling Awareness

Long before children learn to spell, they become aware that words are composed of alphabet letters. As they spot alphabet letters and words in their environment and begin experimenting with them, children see that some of their efforts are readable and some are not. They develop an awareness that there is a consistency and order about the way in which alphabet letters form words.

There are two essential concepts about spelling that a child must understand before any instruction makes sense. Spelling is consistent, and one word can represent a number of people. One child discovered this while writing greeting cards with a friend. The friend wrote (and spelled aloud) D-A-D-D-Y. The younger child exclaimed, "Why that's the way I spell *my* daddy's name!" The child had learned two things: the word "Daddy" is written the same way no matter who writes it and the word is spelled the same way no matter whose daddy it refers to. Until children grasp these concepts, they rightfully believe that each time somebody writes a word it is generated anew. They see no reason for studying the word carefully because the next time someone writes it, the word will be different.

A child who is developing spelling awareness notices how words are spelled. First, he notices initial consonants and can be heard to discover, "L is for Larry and for Linda." He notices that some words are longer than others, and he asks adults to spell words for him. Each of these behaviors indicates that the child is approaching the point where he can learn how to spell words on his own.

How Spelling Develops

Young children are learning to spell long before they receive any instruction. They come to school and to writing with an impressive array of knowledge about our language.

You can compare learning to spell with learning to talk. At first, a baby babbles just as the young child scribbles and pretends to write. While the child may be aware that words are spelled, that awareness is not yet in evidence. The child attempts to write (play writing) and may even "read" what is written, but the concept that spelling is involved in writing has not yet developed.

Children learning to talk next enter a phase called holophrase. They utter one word, but that one word stands for an entire sentence or thought ("Mama" means, "Mommy, I want to get up"). In spelling, the equivalent stage is one-letter spelling. One or two letters represent entire sentences or phrases. Some term this the primitive or deviant stage because, at first, the letters have no resemblance to the words they represent, but they are recognizable alphabet letters. Shortly, however, in the pre-phonetic stage, letters begin to bear some resemblance to those in the word or words they represent. "DiulDD" may represent "Daddy," or "DFRGBM" may represent "Daddy took me for a ride in the car." Skye's message, "Once upon a time there was a monster . . . and a house and a little girl . . . ." is barely decipherable in illustration 77.

Illustration 77

Usually, children learn to spell initial consonants first, final consonants second, and medial consonants third. Vowels appear in spelling after consonants do. That is understandable because most words are easily recognized by their consonants alone (M-TH-R is clearly Mother). Children's spellings, at this point, represent abbreviated forms, with consonants playing the central role. **Dg** for dog, **ct** for cat, **bd** for birthday, and **mk** for milk are common pre-phonetic spellings.

Summer's letter to Santa in illustration 78 is a bit more legible than Skye's because Summer has begun to use some vowels to spell words.

"Dear Santa, I love you. I hope you have fun riding in your sleigh. Bring me lots of presents please. I will leave out some cookies with milk. Love Summer"

As they move into phonetic spelling, children add vowels to their words so that they appear as more completed words. The vowels are not correct, but the message can be read. Which nursery rhyme follows?

jak bee nibl jak bee cik jak japt oavr a cadl stk.

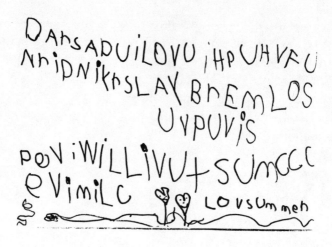

Illustration 78

Which popular Christmas song?

DASID THRER THA SANO
IN A ONI HROS APIN SALA
AVR THE ELS WE GO
LAF IN AL THE WAY
BALLS ON BABTALS RIG
MAK IN SPIRS BRID
AIW WAT FUN IT IS TORID
AND SIG A SLAIN SG TO NIT
JIGL BALLS JIGL BALLS
JIGL AL THE WAY

It is not hard to decipher the stories in illustrations 79 and 80. "Once upon a time there was a mouse and a dog and they were tired so they went to bed." "Once upon a time there was a ghost in my house and I was scared of him. He scared my Mommy, too. And my dogs too And Denise and Joey."

wuns a puna tim ther wuz a maous
Dog and thay war tuiyard #Sow thay wit to and a
Bid

Illustration 79

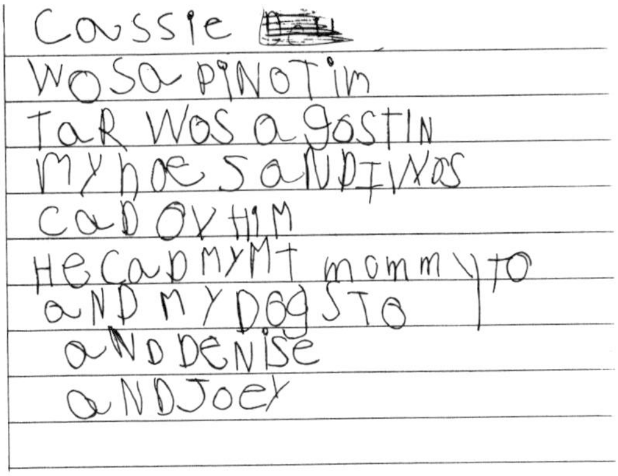

Illustration 80

Shane wrote the short story in illustration 79. Compare Shane's spelling of "Once upon a time," with Cassie's and Mitchel's in illustrations 80 and 81.

"Once upon a time there was an old house and the (dog) had puppies and the cat had babies."

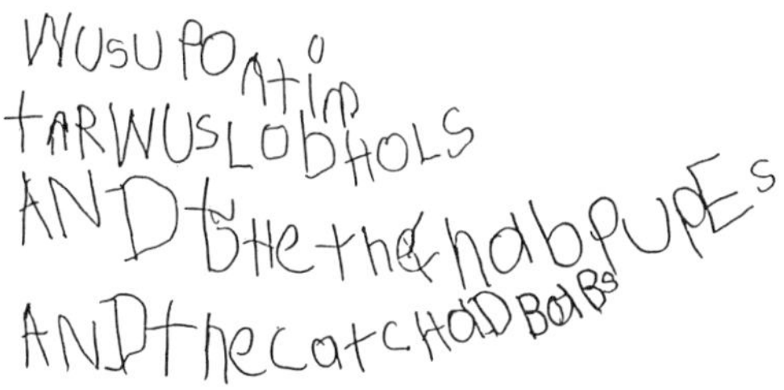

Illustration 81

As children acquire knowledge of consonant blends (two consonants together), they place vowels in their words. The initial consonant may take the place of the blend:

cals for class

genn for green

tip for trip

Blends coming at the end of the word are even harder to hear and to spell, resulting in:

dot for don't

wat for want

pot for post

angy for angry

At about this time, children begin to become aware that longer words need more letters than shorter words. Their spelling takes what looks like a backward step as they write **cr** for car, **snagfdrpmn** for snowman. Snowman needs more letters, so children abstractly insert them, but later the letters come closer to the correct ones.

Parallel with this development in spelling is your child's expanded vocabulary of frequently used words that are memorized, and therefore, spelled perfectly. Naturally, the first correct spelling is usually your child's name, then the names of family members. In illustration 82 Steve drew a picture and wrote about his sisters and brothers. Because he wrote about his family, he could spell every word but "smart" and "except." Katie is obviously the littlest and not smart yet.

I Love Doug and Jill and Katie.

I like Doug and Jill and Katie.

all of you Are smot itxsopt Katie.

Illustration 82

Frequently used words follow. Children learn to spell "Dear" and "Love" if they write letters; they spell "Happy New Year," etc., if they write greeting cards; they spell the names of items such as "dog," "cat," "tree," and "house" if they label pictures. Then, when children write messages, they learn common basic words, such as "and," "the," "so," and "but."

Vowels are the last letters that children learn to use correctly. What may appear to be haphazard spelling of vowels at this stage shows, on closer inspection, how very astute children are. Long vowels, such as the **a** in lake, most beginning

---

writers will spell by its letter name. Short vowels, such as the **e** in net, children spell with the long vowel that sounds the closest and is made in a similar place in the mouth and throat. Thus, children learning to spell vowels tend to use **a** for short **e, e** for short **i, i** for short **o,** and **o** for short **u.** They are often interchanged haphazardly at first because their sounds are unemphasized in speech and often hard to differentiate.

A step in learning to speak is the use of simple rules. Similarly, children begin to use simple rules to spell. This level of spelling development is called transitional spelling. Children who can read learn to use spelling rules quickly. Common early rules include those for some sound/symbol relationships. Children spell all the "at" words (cat, fat, bat, etc.). They learn to use the plural **s; ed,** or **d** for past tense, and **ing.**

One element common to both speaking and spelling is overgeneralization. Children say, "He runned after me," instead of using the irregular past tense, "He ran." They have internalized the rule, but are applying it to more cases than those in which it works. Similarly, young spellers rely on rules which applied in previous spellings but yield errors due to the inconsistency of the English language. Examples include:

BALIE (ballet)
BOTED (bought)
FREETOUS (Fritos)
JANUWARY (January)
LETUS (lettuce)
MILLYONS (millions)
TOYLET PAPER (toilet paper)

In these cases, the spellings make logical sense. While we think such overgeneralizations are "cute," they represent real freedom on the part of novice spellers. For the first time, children are taking risks with spelling new words and using rules that have worked in the past. It is very important, therefore, not to correct or criticize spellings of this type.

Gradually, children move into more precise spelling just as they moved into more precise speech. None of the steps listed above is a clearly defined stage, for all overlap and interact. Some words are easier to learn than others, but what is amazing is the tremendous amount of thought that goes into children's beginning efforts at spelling.

After children have learned simple rules, their most consistent errors are overgeneralizations. Therefore, it is important to avoid asking your child to "sound out" spelling words. Instead, suggest that he look at the word to study it. Phonetic spellers are some of the worst adult spellers. You can read what they spell but their "spelling sense" is inadequate. Proofreading and looking for spelling errors help a child learn to recognize the inconsistent spellings of the English language. Further, many common sounds in the English language have multiple spellings. The long **e** for example, is spelled in at least fourteen different ways.

Children are ready for formal spelling instruction when they reach the correct spelling stage. In illustration 83 Lauren made only four spelling errors in her story. She omitted the **n** from the **nt** blend in "hunting." She spelled "honey" with a double consonant, perhaps because words with short vowel sounds are usually followed by doubled consonants. She wrote

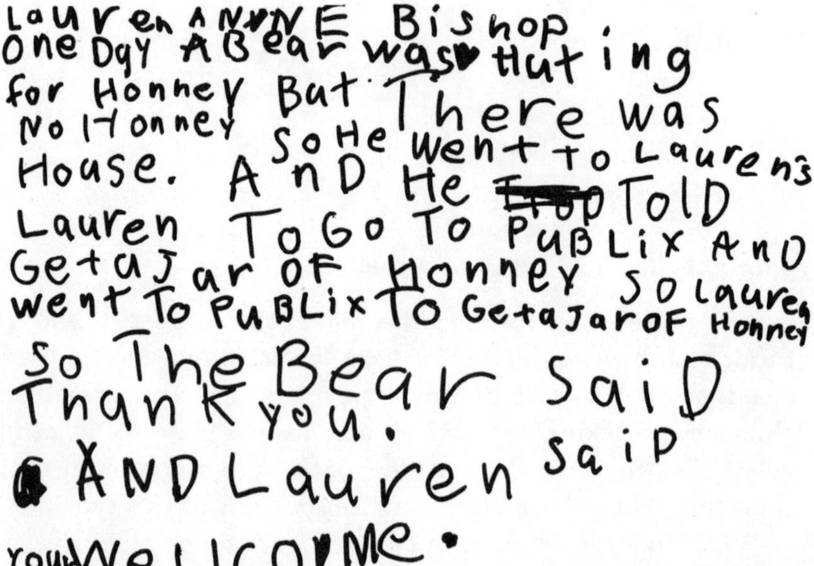

Illustration 83

Growing Up Writing

the wrong homonym for "you're." And she made a compound word out of "welcome" (wellcome) which may reflect the origin of the word. The latter three errors are all logical—the types of errors children in the correct spelling stage make.

Spelling Progressions

Level I
Spelling Awareness
- Words are made up of alphabet letters.
- Spelling is consistent; words don't change the way they are spelled.
- No matter who writes a word or what type or print is used, the word is spelled the same way.

Level II
Primitive (or Deviant) Spelling
- Random letters represent words.
- There is no relationship between spelling and the word it represents.
- Numbers and alphabet letters are differentiated.

Level III
Pre-phonetic (Consonant) Spelling
- The initial consonant or a few consonants represent the whole word.
- Some consonants match their sounds.
- The spelling is very hard to read, but decipherable if you know the code.
- Initial and final consonants become correct.
- Some initial and final blends become correct.
- Longer words have longer spellings.

Level IV
Phonetic Spelling
- There is an almost perfect match between letters and sounds.
- Some sight words are spelled correctly.
- Overgeneralizations occur.
- Some vowels are used as markers, but are often incorrect.
- A passage is rather easy to read.

Level V
Transitional Spelling
- Words look a lot more like English.
- More vowels are used.
- Common letter patterns, such as **oo, ou, ng, igh,** and **ck** appear, but not always in the right places.
- Inflectional endings such as **ed, ing,** and **s** appear.

Level VI
Correct Spelling
- The child is ready for formal spelling instruction.
- Most words are spelled correctly except for individual words which need to be practiced.

Common Misspellings

There are many strategies that are used to spell a word. One is by the sound of alphabet letters as in: LSA (Elsa) and IVRE (Ivory). Another is to sound out blends so slowly that a vowel sound is added as in PALAY (play) and BOROWN (brown)

Children may misspell a word because they are trying to spell it the way it looks, as in TEH (the), BAOOLNS (balloons), PAES (peas), and WAHT (what).

Children may confuse meaning with spelling (since meaning is a good clue to spelling some words) and come up with a spelling like AXLACUTED for executed.

Inaccurate pronunciations or inarticulate speech results in misspellings such as PATATAS (potatoes), YOGAT (yogurt), ORNUGS (oranges), and TOLE (told). Allison drew a picture of her favorite fairy tale and labeled it "Allison Wonderland."

Some spelling errors occur when a syllable is left out of the pronunciation of a word like BARBRA (Barbara) or VEGTBLLS (vegetables).

Because they first concentrate on the beginnings of words, children often misspell word endings, as in BUTTR (butter), TRND (turned), and MIDL (middle). When they do learn rules for adding endings they overgeneralize them as is seen in GOINING (going), MERRERY (Merry), HAVEING (having).

Homophones (words that sound the same, but are spelled differently) cause problems for advanced spellers. Children must learn these by sight. Reading improves children's ability to spell these words:

aisle/isle	creak/creek	meat/meet
ant/aunt	dear/deer	pair/pare/pear
ball/bawl	doe/dough	pain/pane
bare/bear	eight/ate	rain/reign
be/bee	eye/I	right/write
beet/beat	its/it's	rose/rows
berry/bury	fir/fur	sea/see
blue/blew	flea/flee	soar/sore
buy/by	flower/flour	stake/steak
cent/scent/sent	hair/hare	sun/son
cereal/serial	hear/here	to/too/two
cheap/cheep	knew/new/gnu	toad/towed
chili/chilly	know/no	vain/vane/vein
close/clothes	knight/night	wood/would

There are times when children avoid writing words or modify the words they write to avoid their spelling deficiencies. Witness the child who wrote "Happy Mommy Day" because she could not yet spell "Mother."

It is important to remember that children are actively thinking when they are spelling. It is this thought that makes children good spellers in the long run. If you correct your child's spelling errors, he'll probably stop guessing or inventing spellings and start relying on your help for spelling. He may use only those words that he can surely spell correctly in his writing. Failure to take spelling risks results in dull writing.

Overcompensation for spelling errors is counterproductive. Therefore, it is important to focus on the content of what your child writes and not on the form, at least until the final draft is perfected in all other ways and is ready for mailing or other public display. Then, together with your child, you can help make spelling more precise, rather than "corrected."

Older children who want to expand their repertoire of difficult words can make a spelling notebook, dictionary, or card file to list those words they want to learn to spell accurately. You might give them a list of the most frequently misspelled words in the English language.

The old-fashioned idea of writing spelling words ten times

each is of little value in learning to spell because children do it mechanically and without thought. If your child learns things especially well visually, he should look at the word carefully; if he learns more easily by listening he should spell the word aloud; and if he learns more easily by touching he should write it. In addition, it helps if children notice whether or not the word follows general rules of spelling.

How Spelling Is Taught in School

Spelling instruction in many classrooms consists of memorizing a list of words either from a basal textbook or a teacher-generated list for a test on Friday. Words are generally grouped according to the spelling of specific sounds, though some texts have pages of sight words interspersed throughout. Sometimes, children take a pre-test on Monday so that they only need to learn those words they initially missed.

The problems with such an approach to spelling are twofold. First, it divorces spelling from the writing process. Children may not use the words they are studying in their compositions. Some teachers either supplement basal spelling programs or replace them with words children misspell in the compositions. You can examine any original writing your child brings home from school to select words for a word box or homemade dictionary. Limit a list to a very few words a week, but you can expect mastery of those words.

A second problem with total reliance on a basal for spelling instruction is that if the words are presented only using generalizations and letter/sound correspondence, children may grow to overemphasize sound in their approaches to spelling. They'll spell words phonetically all the time rather than use a balance between sound and sight. Newer spelling series suggest that children use many different modalities when learning how to spell a word. The Zaner-Bloser Spelling Series suggests the following procedure:

Look at the word.
Say the word.
Spell the word.
Write the word.
Check the word.

This approach maximizes your child's opportunity for learning to spell and would be a good system for him to use for learning spelling bank words as well.

Some teachers have individualized spelling lists for each child in the class. As children revise their writing, they find words that are misspelled and add them to a personal collection of words to learn. Teachers who individualize their spelling programs emphasize memorizing individual words. You may not want to leave your child's development to those words he happens to misspell in his writing. You can find a list of spelling generalizations and be sure your children are learning how to apply them. In addition, a spelling textbook teaches other skills which are often not taught systematically elsewhere in the curriculum: capitalizing, alphabetizing, proofreading, and even vocabulary development. These, of course, can be taught as a part of writing programs, but they do need systematic attention somewhere in the program.

In the primary grades, some teachers provide all of the spellings children request as they write. This can cause children to rely too much on the adult crutch and avoid spelling on their own. You'll want to be sure that children have opportunities to compose independently without adult assistance. Children who won't write words they cannot spell develop far more slowly as composers.

A major goal of a spelling program is to teach children to recognize their own spelling errors. You can teach your child to underline the words in his stories that he is not sure are spelled right. From these underlined words, you can see that even though a word is spelled correctly, your child has not mastered it. Much of the writing your child naturally does at home is for other people and therefore needs to be proofread carefully.

A strong spelling program balances learning words by sight, sound, and writing. It balances learning words missed in compositions and words which fit spelling generalizations. If you are aware of the school's spelling program, you can augment it at home to provide a balanced program for your children. You can monitor your children's progress by observing (and even recording) the errors they make in their spontaneous writings. While it is important not to point out these errors directly to children who are not fluent writers, spelling mistakes do indicate where study is needed.

Spelling Problems

If your child is having problems with spelling, inquire about how spelling is being taught in school. The problem may be related to learning modalities. Children who have visual and kinesthetic learning strengths may have difficulty learning sound/symbol relationships. Children who have auditory strengths may not be looking at words carefully enough. If the basal approach used in the classroom relies solely on auditory approaches to learning spelling words, you can compensate at home by giving your children words from their writing to learn by sight. Children who are kinesthetic learners may not have enough opportunities to write words or manipulate alphabet letters into words.

You'll need to be sure that your child's spelling problems do not contribute to a lack of interest in writing, for it is only as children become active and eager writers that they have opportunities to develop their spelling skills. Children at school may not see the relevance of learning how to spell an abstract list of words each week. Attitude toward learning is important.

Most children who are poor spellers write words phonetically. They need to develop their observational skills by both reading and revising their writing until they can recognize how words look when they are spelled correctly.

Parental Help in Spelling

Should you spell words for your child as he is writing? When you provide spellings, you suggest to your child that he cannot write independently. It is better to urge your child to spell words the best he can. While he is spelling on his own, he is actively thinking in ways which make him a better speller in the long run. Only if your child gets frustrated by not being able to spell should you offer help. And then, be sure there are times when your child writes when you aren't available to help.

When you do spell words for your child, it is helpful to write the word on a slip of paper, a card, or in a spelling dictionary while you spell it aloud. If you draw a faint line on the paper first (if the paper is unlined,) your child can see the relationship of letters above and below the line. Writing the word lets your child see the word and is especially important if the child is a visual learner. Besides, it's hard to remember all the letters when they are spelled out loud. If possible, spell the word in syllables or in logical parts to help your child memorize the word.

Children who are just learning to write usually ask to have words spelled. Since they are writing very slowly anyway, stopping to have a word spelled doesn't usually hinder their message. When children revise their stories, however, it makes more sense to write the entire story with invented spellings, then return and get accurate spellings. They can take their time looking up the words in a dictionary.

In order to look up words easily in a dictionary, your child must be able to alphabetize quickly and must know initial consonant sounds. If children have not yet developed these two skills, looking words up in a dictionary takes so long that it is not worth the effort. Instead, they can ask for adult help on the final revision. To speed up the development of dictionary skills, your child can play games to see how fast he can find a word. You can see who can find the word first—your child using a child's dictionary or you using an adult dictionary. Your child learns approximately where in the alphabet initial letters are located and turns immediately to the beginning, the middle, or the end of the book.

Children enjoy looking up their friends' names, addresses, and phone numbers in a telephone book. You can make phone books or address books for your child to use, listing the names alphabetically. Then your child can practice alphabetizing skills in other ways.

Dictionaries and Word Cards

As your child is learning to spell, he might enjoy making a personal dictionary. You can make a spelling dictionary by taking a small spiral-bound notebook and notching each page with a letter of the alphabet. You or your child can write new or difficult words on the appropriate pages. If you attach a pencil to the dictionary, when your child needs a word, you can easily write it down for him.

Word cards work in much the same way, but it is harder to find them without alphabetical headings and they can easily get lost. Younger children who want to copy words find word cards very helpful for repetitious messages such as greeting cards. Your child can save word cards for spelling practice.

Once your child begins to revise his work by writing rough drafts and then checking their spelling and punctuation, it is time to provide him with a high-quality dictionary. There are several such children's dictionaries available. *The Macmillan Dictionary for Children* (Morris, Christopher G., Editor. New York: 1982), and *Webster's Beginning Dictionary* (G. & C. Merriam Company, Massachusetts: 1980), are examples of high-quality children's dictionaries.

Spelling Games

There are many commercial games that help children become better spellers. Spelling words out loud or manipulating them in a game can help children learn how to spell new words and develop positive attitudes toward spelling.

Several games have players manipulate alphabet letters to spell words. In "Spill and Spell"® you make words out of dice with letters on them. "Scrabble"® is a board game—you build words out of letters in crossword puzzle fashion, scoring points for long words or using hard letters. In "Hangman,"® children use paper and pencil to build words by guessing which letters might fit in the allotted spaces. "Probe,"® likewise, has players guess hidden alphabet letters to reveal words.

Word-find games are especially useful for teaching children to proofread for spelling errors. Some come in workbook form, like "See-A-Word."® Others have variations; like "Boggle,"® a timed version with dice.

There are several popular electronic games, such as "Speak and Spell."® In this game, the computer asks the player to punch out the spelling of the word on a typewriter-like keyboard and then corrects the work. Similarly, there are spelling games for home computers. "Instant Zoo"® includes a word-scramble game which reveals a letter at a time in mixed-up order. Children can make their own lists to use in "Word Scramble,"® using a text editor.

You can make up games which involve spelling. Little children enjoy manipulating plastic magnetic letters into words on the refrigerator door. Pencil and paper games such as "Pair Tree" involve players in thinking up homonym pairs. Long car rides provide another opportunity for oral spelling games that help children learn letter sounds. While driving in a car you might begin to look for words that begin with the same sound. You can make the game harder by selecting only words in one category, such as fruits, flowers, birds, vehicles, or animals. Tongue twisters, finger plays, and riddles provide another type of oral language word play that helps children learn the letter sounds.

Poor Spellers

Nothing turns children off to writing more than being unable to spell or write their thoughts on paper. Children who can't spell well usually avoid writing, which hampers their development in other areas of learning as well. It is important to help poor spellers gain confidence through a gradual program of remediation.

Spelling is linked to reading. Children who read a lot are usually good spellers. Spelling is also linked to listening. Children need to be able to hear the sounds as well as visually remember what words look like. Therefore, anything you can do to increase the amount of reading and listening to stories, poetry, and songs, will help a poor speller.

You'll need to set aside time for learning a few words a week. Take the words from your child's writing and develop a systematic way to record the words he has learned—a card file or spelling notebook. Find out how the child learns best—by sound, by sight, by touch or by a combination of these—and emphasize that approach. Help your child learn generalizations such as, "i before e, except after c, or when sounded like a, as in neighbor and weigh."

Finally, help change your child's attitude toward spelling by emphasizing successes rather than by pointing out errors. Keep charts or graphs of progress. Assist in spelling when your child requests help.

Poor spellers can camouflage their disability if they can

recognize their errors. Teaching a poor speller to proofread and to use a dictionary is critical. Don't forget the lighthearted approach to spelling through games! Word-find games are especially helpful for poor spellers.

Proofreading Spelling

As readers, we make mental corrections in spelling in order to read for meaning. We become so engrossed in the content of what we are reading that we are likely to overlook errors in form, thereby making accurate proofreading very difficult. What works for some children is to "read" the piece backwards— to look at each word from the end to the beginning to see if it is spelled correctly. That way, it is impossible to read for meaning and the proofreader is forced to look at spellings. Finding one's own errors is a most critical skill, and it takes practice.

If proofreading the entire piece alone is overwhelming, you can help by placing a mark (-) in the margin next to the line where there is a spelling error. That way the child only has to hunt through one line of writing to find the error.

Chapter 8

Punctuation, Capitalization, and Usage

"**P**unctuation makes my writing talk, doesn't it?"
"The rule for making capitals is to capitalize the important words, like Mommy, Daddy, Teacher, Ice Cream, and God."
"I just writted what I thinked!"
"Dad, you need a catastrophe (apostrophe) there!"

Punctuation and capitalization skills, like spelling, take a long time to perfect. You won't want to pay attention to them until your children are fluent writers, and then only in the revision and proofreading process. Punctuation and, to a lesser degree, capitalization, influence the legibility of a piece of writing. It is punctuation that puts words into meaningful units for readers.

Punctuation Awareness

Children develop an awareness of punctuation in the same way that they develop awareness of writing and spelling, through interaction with writing. As they learn to read, they notice punctuation marks. As they write or as adults write for them, they see punctuation in action.

Very young children incorporate commas, periods, and apostrophes into their scribbles and pretend writing. Young writers use exclamation points early and vigorously. In Jennifer's two-page story (illustration 84), the only punctuation she uses is exclamation points. Teaching young children punctuation rules is counterproductive because the rules are abstract. Actually punctuating their work gives it flair. Children enjoy *using* punctuation; they don't enjoy studying it.

at nigt I went to
bed and I heard
a nose and I got up
and thrnd the
ligt on an it was
my cat and I went Back
to bed and teny I felt something!!
it was my cat Plaing with
my ear
in the midl of the
nigt and I coing
Go to bed and I told
my mommy and She
said I will see
and She said
Go Back to bed
and I did
The end

Illustration 84

Children discover commas when they write personal letters and see commas in use. They learn about periods when they write more than one sentence, and question marks when they ask a question (The classic is "How are you?" in a letter). They learn about apostrophes when people label their things— Bob's coat.

Helping Children Learn to Punctuate Properly

Children learn to punctuate by writing and seeing the need for punctuation and by learning to proofread their work. Typically, punctuation is the last consideration in completing a piece of writing. After an author has written the content, the mechanics of spelling, punctuation, and capitalization are perfected.

Periods
Punctuation indicates how a piece is read aloud. Periods tell you where to pause in your reading. Before children use periods, they sometimes begin each sentence on a new line even if they don't use punctuation, as Darrel has done in illustration 85.

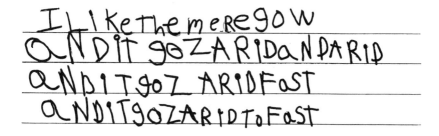

Illustration 85

"I like the merry-go-round and it goes around and around and it goes around fast and it goes around too fast."

When children first notice periods, they may put one after each word they write. They think that periods separate words. Andrea put a period after each word when she wrote, "I like school because it's fun," in illustration 86.

Sometimes, children place periods at the end of each line of writing. Lots of easy reading books do print one sentence on a line, and early childhood teachers often make charts that way. Small wonder, then, that young children first think that the "rule" for using periods is at the end of each line of writing. That is where periods most frequently appear in the material that they read.

Illustration 86

J.R. wrote (illustration 87): "I like cats and they are my favorite animals And I like dogs. And they are my favorite animals, too and I like school and books."

One first grader was writing the second line of a story when she started to crinkle up her paper to throw it away, saying "I messed up." Her mother asked what happened and the child explained that her sentence had ended in the middle of a line, and she had gone on writing instead of starting on a new line. Her mother explained that, in books, sentences often end that way. She showed her a picture book that had continuous writing onto another page.

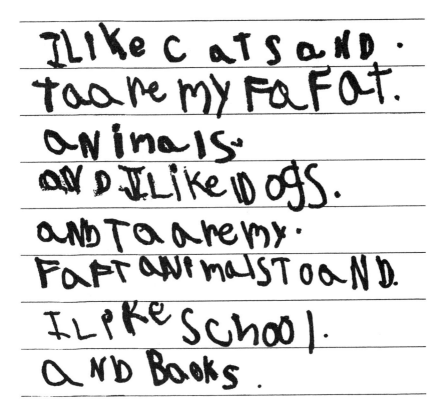

Illustration 87

Children who read a lot are less likely to make this error. They have seen real books where periods occur throughout the line whenever a sentence ends. Children who are just learning to use periods exaggerate the period (and dots above **i**'s) in size.

Periods are used to end statements. Examples of periods used in young children's writings include statements such as "For you." One child put a period after each item in a list (illustration 88). It was as though she were answering questions such as, "What do we need at the store?" "Bread." Or, "What do you want for Christmas?" "A doll."

School-age children who are beginning to be prolific writers often write with run-on sentences, circumventing the need for periods. ("I went to the store and I rode my bike and I put the groceries in my basket and . . . "). If your child uses run-on sentences, have him read his final drafts aloud and,

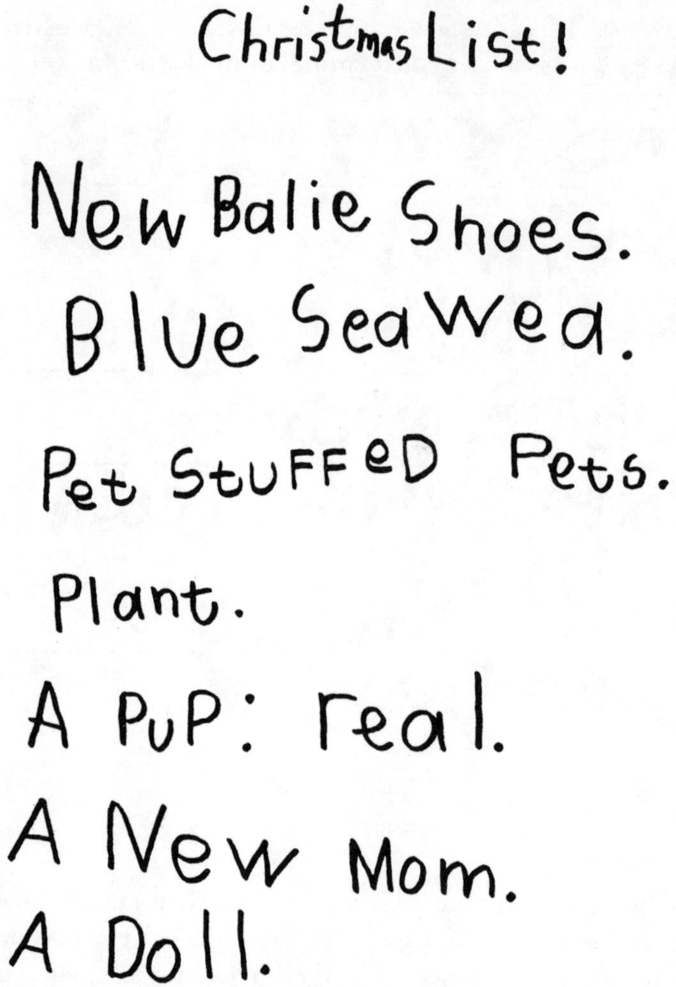

Christmas List!

New Balie Shoes.
Blue SeaWea.

Pet StuFFeD Pets.

Plant.

A PuP: real.

A New Mom.
A Doll.

Illustration 88

whenever he pauses for a breath or for emphasis, add punctuation. He learns to cross out all of the connecting "ands" and replace them with periods. You can have your child tape record the piece as another way to hear where the terminal punctuation should go. As the tape is played back, he can follow the words and listen to where punctuation is needed.

Exclamation Points
Practically from the start, children write sentences that need

forms of punctuation other than periods. First, they learn that there are different types of terminal punctuation, as shown by the child who wrote:

Do not come in!

Illustration 89

The child knew that this statement placed on a door was more emphatic than most but did not know the distinction between a question mark and an exclamation point. So, she invented a mark which was a combination of the two.

Illustration 90

Very young children readily use exclamation points as in illustrations 90 and 91. Practically everything they write is exciting (at least to them), so there is a natural need to give emphasis to their statements. Sometimes they achieve emphasis by repeating words as in illustration 92. Later, children learn that the exclamation point adds emphasis, so they no longer need the extra words.

Illustration 91

Illustration 92

Growing Up Writing

Repetition of letters adds emphasis:

"To yoooul!"

Young writers also show emphasis by enlarging the size of the letters:

I am Five NOW!

They also underline for emphasis, as in "The Magic Garden" story in illustration 93.

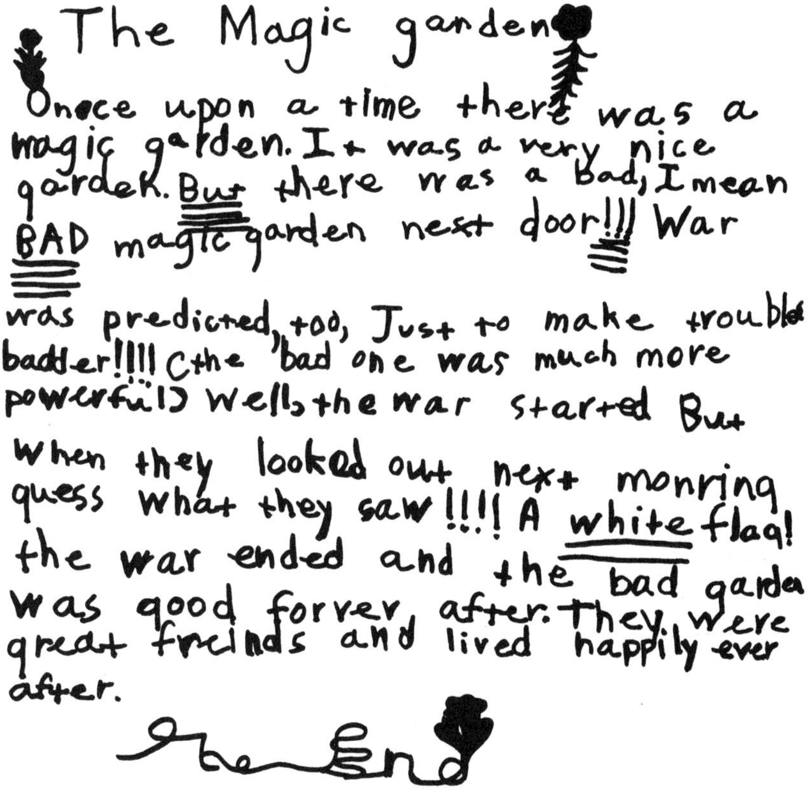

The Magic garden
Once upon a time there was a magic garden. It was a very nice garden. But there was a bad, I mean BAD magic garden next door!!! War was predicted, too, Just to make trouble badder!!!! (the 'bad' one was much more powerful) well, the war started But when they looked out next monring guess what they saw !!!! A white flag! the war ended and the bad garden was good forvev, after. They were great freinds and lived happily ever after.

The End

Illustration 93

The following exclamations were made by one young writer:

It was wonderful! (in friendly letters)

You can be my friend!

HI! (labels to pictures)

Meow!

Come to a party! (in an invitation)

I got lots! Well I got lots of leaves! I got a stone!
Oh la la! (doodles)
Welcome home to Mom! (on a sign)
Oh Dummy! (on an unhappy note to a parent)
You found it! (at the end of a treasure hunt)

Each indicates, at appropriate times, enthusiasm or emphasis on the part of the writer.

Question Marks

Question marks, similarly, are noticeable enough so that children easily learn to place them at the end of questions when they're writing. Though question marks do not appear as often in writing as exclamation points, they do occur in children's writing. When writing friendly letters, children ask, "How are you?" and they expect to receive answers in the mail. Friendly letters and notes generate other substantive questions as well. For example:"Do you like this letter?" "Will you be my friend?" "How is Aunt Samantha?" "When are you coming to visit?" Invitations contain questions. And children merely write the questions they might ask orally, hoping that their writing will result in a more favorable response. "Dad, could we have lunch on the shed roof?" is an example.

Valentine's Day is the perfect holiday for a study of question marks. Practically every valentine contains at least one question and probably an exclamation point as well (illustration 94).

Commas

Commas have many uses. In friendly letters, commas come after the greeting and in the closing. Children just memorize these uses. Children who write letters copy the adult model of placing commas appropriately. You can hear the need for commas in a series when you read a piece aloud. Long before they use commas in a series, children write "ands" in their place. Commas make oral reading easier. Children sense this and write endings such as: "Well, I've got to go now," or "Well, got to say goodbye now." Notes to an individual contain commas in direct address, a rather sophisticated usage, yet so related to oral reading children easily learn it. Since commas have so many

Illustration 94

uses, children have more opportunities to use them by writing in a variety of different ways. Children first writing commas may use slashes (/) or hyphens (-) until they perceive the comma accurately. This is true for other punctuation marks as well. When in doubt, they use a hyphen.

In the first paragraph of a friendly letter (illustration 95), one child uses seven different punctuation marks: three uses for commas, eight periods, two question marks, one apostrophe, one colon, eleven hyphens, and an exclamation point!

You can see why writing letters is a great way to learn punctuation!

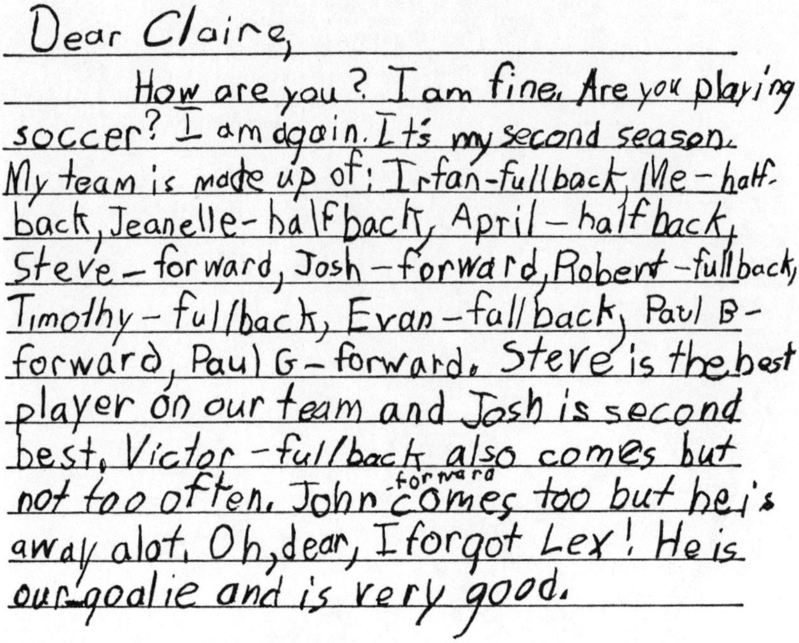

> Dear Claire,
>
> How are you? I am fine. Are you playing soccer? I am again. It's my second season. My team is made up of: Irfan-fullback, Me-half-back, Jeanelle-halfback, April-halfback, Steve-forward, Josh-forward, Robert-fullback, Timothy-fullback, Evan-fullback, Paul B-forward, Paul G-forward. Steve is the best player on our team and Josh is second best. Victor-fullback also comes but not too often. John-forward comes too but he's away alot. Oh, dear, I forgot Lex! He is our goalie and is very good.

Illustration 95

Apostrophes

The best way for your child to learn words that have apostrophes is by sight. Rather than explain that **can't** stands for **cannot** and that the apostrophe replaces the **o**, it is easier to learn to spell the word **can't**, complete with apostrophe. The origin of contractions can be explained later in the upper elementary grades or if children question them. Children may not form the apostrophe correctly at first. They become aware that one is needed, then work on the way it is formed. Witness one child's development of the use of an apostrophe in illustration 96.

Quotation Marks

Quotation marks are used when children are writing captions to comics, interviews, or fictional narratives where the characters speak.

Colons

Colons are used when people list things. A child listed "A pup: real," on her Christmas list. She labeled a drawing, "My cat.

Dot' no-T w e\ve

I Ve\ Do-T

I\ve

Robin Redbreast's Comin' home!

Valentine's

Illustration 96

Nickname: TishTosh." Children enjoy writing memos.

> To: Dad
> From: Marni
> Don't forget the glue.

Children whose parents work in offices see memos in use. Shortly after his mother's secretary sent a note on memo paper, Kyle sent all of his artwork "To: Karla, From: Kyle." Gradually he changed his terminology to "For Karla From Kyle," and dropped the use of the colon.

Other Punctuation Marks
One young child wrote to a friend, "Your grade is 'A'," complete

with single quotation marks around the A (illustration 97). Where had the child learned that? From observing it written somewhere. In illustration 98, another wrote, "Oh Dummy . . . . . . !" Were those dots periods or ellipsis points?

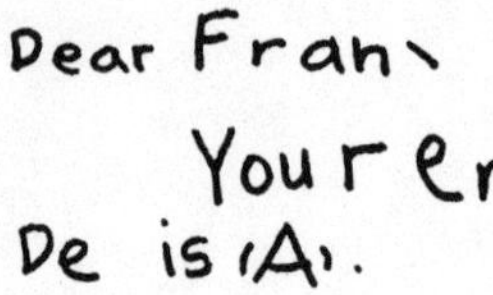

Dear Fran

You r era-
De is 'A'.

Oh Du mmy......!

Illustration 97   *Illustration 98*

Kristy got carried away with her use of parentheses when describing the five art projects she entered in an art contest (illustration 99).

Nobody had ever taught these children to use punctuation

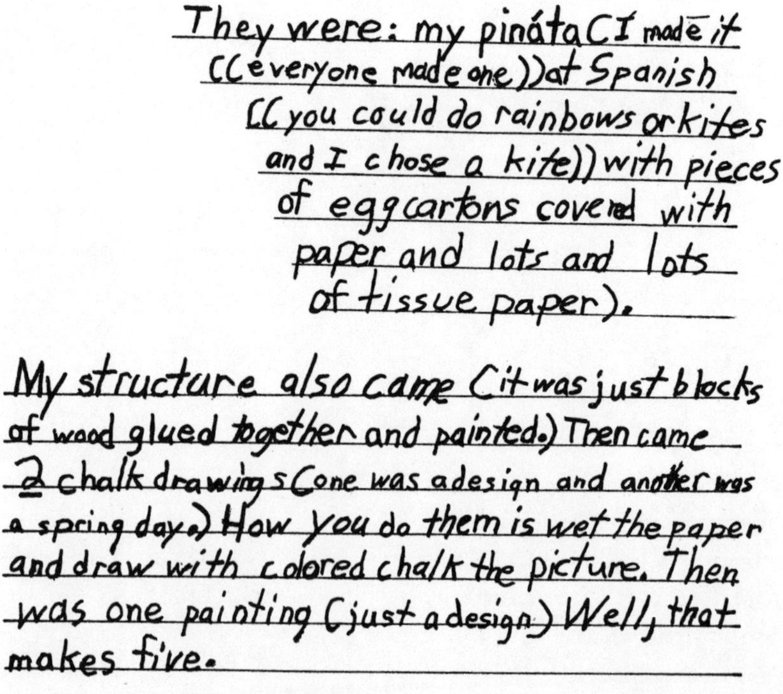

They were: my pináta CI made it
CCeveryone made one))at Spanish
CC you could do rainbows or kites
and I chose a kite)) with pieces
of egg cartons covered with
paper and lots and lots
of tissue paper).

My structure also came Cit was just blocks
of wood glued together and painted.) Then came
2 chalk drawings Cone was a design and another was
a spring day.) How you do them is wet the paper
and draw with colored chalk the picture. Then
was one painting Cjust a design) Well, that
makes five.

Illustration 99

but it appeared in their writing correctly! It makes no sense t
teach children all of the minor forms of punctuation until the,
are actually ready to use them in their own writing. As we help
children refine their work, we can mention the punctuation at
appropriate times.

Hyphens

Children learn hyphenated words by sight as though the
hyphen were an alphabet letter. "Jack-in-the-box" wrote one
child who was becoming aware of hyphens.

Possessives

Often, children confuse possessives and plurals. They use an
apostrophe each time they write the plural form of a word.
Possessives are easier to understand if you ask whose boots
those are rather than try to explain that possessives are the
shortened form of "the boots of Mary," which you don't hear in
normal speech.

Proofreading

To help your child know what to look for as he proofreads for
punctuation, give him the parts of the following checklist that
he needs.

1. End punctuation
Did you put a period, question mark, or exclamation point after
each sentence?
2. Commas
Did you put a comma between words in a series?
Did you use a comma to set off extra words, such as "yes," or
names used in direct address (Sure, Sally, I'll come)? Did you use
a comma before or after quotation marks?
3. Quotation marks
Did you use quotation marks to set off the exact words of a
speaker?
4. Apostrophes
Did you use an apostrophe in contractions: let's, can't, don't?
Did you use an apostrophe in possessives:
singular—Jim's, child's, dog's   plural—trains', cats', peoples'

The POllACKATOO

Once upon a time there was a pollackATOO. she was a very nice pollackatoo. Her name was Feather. Her mistress was called star Rose Laneada. Now the pollackatoo could talk. one Day they were out on a walk. They (The pollackatoo and star) had walked Quite far when they suddenly realized

They were lost! (The pollackatoo could fly too) But the pollackatoo had an ideal. I'll fly up too the tops of the trees with you holding onto my claws and I'll fly you home. Then the pollackatoo took hold of her and they, just when the sun was going down, got home. Then they lived happily ever after.

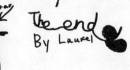

The end
By Laurel

Illustration 100

Don't worry if your child can't explain the rules for punctuation to you. It is **how** he uses punctuation when he writes that counts.

With punctuation as with spelling and handwriting, what is important is that the writing communicates. If your child sees that other people can't read his writing, it will be clear to him that it is important to add punctuation. When children understand the reason why punctuation is important, they more willingly proofread their final drafts than if adults simply tell them to revise.

A child's punctuation development can far exceed instruction. When Laurel wrote the story of the Pollackatoo in illustration 100, she had never received any formal instruction in punctuation. In fact, this was the first story she had written. Laurel was, however, an avid reader and had picked up a lot of information about punctuation from reading.

Writing as an Emotional Outlet

Children find that they can say things in writing that they would not feel comfortable saying out loud. They find that writing adds emphasis to emotional statements.

After her dad refused what one child thought was a reasonable request, she went to her room and wrote, "Dear Dad, I am sorry for you in some ways, in others, not." Another child wrote, "Dummy I hate you." after being refused a request (illustration 101).

Illustration 101

Illustration 102

After an especially trying day, Pam wrote a note to her mom (illustration 102). Positive emotions are powerful in writing. Witness one child's note to a kindergarten teacher in illustration 103.

Illustration 103

Dear Connie

I Love you

I hope that you love me

I am sorry that I cry in the mornings

I really love you Connie

I hope that you really love me

I hope that you have a happy Christmas

Love J.J.

Writing aids children's social interactions with one another. Amy solved a conflict while playing with a friend by writing, "I am vary, vary, vary sore (sorry). Will you be my frind?" Needless to say, the two made up.

Nora, a kindergartner, had the following exchange with Maram, her first grade best friend. Nora had hung up the telephone on Maram, unable to make her understand that she wanted to play at her house and not at Maram's. Maram wrote:

"To Nora!

From Maram!

This is Maram from time you hung up the phone.

(here Maram drew a picture of a sad face)

The end."

When Nora received this note, she ran to her father and asked him to write for her. She then copied the message he had written for her. It said, "Maram, I'm sorry that I hung up the phone on you but I still love you." It ended with a drawing of a happy face. Another child's letter of apology read, "Dear Mom, Please let me go to the game. I am sorry. I love you. P.S. You are nice."

These children found it difficult to offer apologies orally. Their written statements had more impact.

Capitalization

The rules for capitalization in the English language appear rather arbitrary to young learners. Children just learning to write intersperse upper and lowercase letters, depending upon how they've seen adults write. If you write in uppercase letters, your child will. Even if you capitalize correctly, your child may still use uppercase letters in place of lowercase ones. Signs and advertising material tend to be in the uppercase alphabet. Some alphabet letters are easier to make in their uppercase form. Early in their writing, children are not aware that upper and lowercase letters have special functions.

When they first see that uppercase letters serve a function, children typically capitalize each word. The capital letter, rather than a white space between words, makes words distinctive to children. Gradually, they learn to capitalize all but the very common words (and, the, on, to). Then they learn that there are rules for capital letters, and they capitalize words that are important to them, like names, other nouns, and some verbs. In illustration 104, one child shared her apprehension about a class May Pole play, emphasizing the important words by capitalizing them.

MAY DAY!!!!

Tomorrow is it! May Day! Refreshments and everything but, most exciting of all, THE MAY POLE! I hope I do it all right! OOps, here it comes, better get my costume on Later .... YEAY, I DID IT ALLRIGHT !!!!

Illustration 104

The next step is to realize that every sentence begins with a capital letter. Children may confuse this generalization and capitalize the first word of every line until the concept of sentence becomes stronger. Young children rarely use too few capital letters. Rather, they use capitals where they are not needed. Older children, on the other hand, make mistakes in both directions. Some of the hardest capitalization rules to remember are those for capitalizing languages (English), locations (the North, the South, eastern, western), and types of things like breeds of animals (Welsh terrier).

You can best help your child correct mistakes in capitalization during the final proofreading and editing process. By correcting capitalization errors in his own work, your child internalizes the rules for capitalization. He does not need to study formally those rules until he is in the upper elementary grades. Even then, the rules have little impact upon writing unless your child is using the generalizations in his own writings.

Capitalization Checklist for the Use of Fluent Writers Only
(for approximately second grade and up)
1. Did you capitalize the first word in each sentence?
2. Did you capitalize the word "I" each time you used it?
3. Did you capitalize proper names—the special or particular names of:
   people (Tamara, Susan)
   places (United States of America, St. Augustine, Bryce Canyon)
   pets (Winnie, Digger)
   buildings (Fisher Building, Riverfront Stadium)
   streets (Elm Street)
   holidays (Christmas)
   languages (German, French)
   book titles (*Peter Pan*)
   days of the week (Tuesday)
   months of the year (June)
4. Did you capitalize the first word and all important words in the title of your paper (if it has one)?

Dialects and Usage

At first, children write the way they talk. Only after they become accustomed to written language through reading and writing do they notice that written language is different from talk.

People speak in many different dialects. There are regional dialects: Bostonian, Brooklynese, and Southern dialects are easily identifiable. There are cultural dialects. Spanish, Black, and British dialects reflect different cultural backgrounds. And there are social dialects. Sometimes poorer people speak dialects that are different from the dialects of wealthier people, even if they live in the same region. Finally there are personal dialects.

We all speak differently at home and at work. Children speak differently at school, on the playground, and at home.

While these differences may be acceptable in oral speech, there is only one way to write standard English, and children from all backgrounds need to write in this standard form. Some dialect differences can cause errors in usage and spelling if they are written down. For example, the following would be considered usage errors in written English:

repetition of subject—My brother, he rode his bike.

questions without "do"—What you think?

singular noun used with plural modifier—One girl, five girl

incorrect verb tense—He go to work.

incorrect use of "to be"—She be my friend.

same verb for all subjects—I know, you know, he know, we know

Oral language is more relaxed in its enforcement of rules than is written language. To help your child know what usage problems to look for as he proofreads, you might provide the following checklist:

1. Do your verbs agree with their subjects?
   Find your verbs and see.
   (The *apples* in the cart *are* $.50 each.)
   (Here *are* the *books*.)
2. Do your pronouns agree with their antecedents?
   (All *members* should pay *their* dues.)
3. Have you used the correct form for each pronoun?
   (Jimmy and *I* went sailing.)
4. Have you listed yourself last?
   (Tim and *I* laughed.)
5. Have you selected the appropriate homonym?

their, there, they're	*here, hear*
to, too, two	*meat, meet*
its, it's	*no, know*

Editing and Proofreading

Editing and proofreading can be the most tedious of chores or the most exciting part of the writing process for children. If your child's work is going into a homemade storybook collection, is to be displayed on your bulletin board, or is going to be mailed, then he needs to polish it. But editing is pointless if the only people who are going to read the piece are you or a teacher. Why edit a work for the family to read if the content is what is critical? Not every piece of writing should be polished. Some rough drafts need to go in the wastepaper basket. Your child should have the choice about which writings to polish. At home, he'll probably revise business or personal letters, although avid writers will produce stories and poems as well.

You can encourage editing and proofreading when your child starts writing for people outside the family. Keep rough drafts so that your child can see how much improvement has been made.

Your first editing is for content. A discussion of this type of polishing is in the chapter on fluent writers. After the content is refined, then you pay attention to how the piece is written: the spelling, punctuation, capitalization, usage, and, lastly, the handwriting. Your child will probably have to copy the piece over to make its appearance presentable.

You can find punctuation errors by reading the piece aloud. If your child pauses, a comma, period, or some punctuation is needed. By simply noting the spot, he can return to decide upon punctuation after reading the entire work.

Oral reading is not as common in our society as it was in the days prior to television. When members of a family read aloud to each other, they model expressive oral reading. As children learn to be expressive oral readers, they learn to notice punctuation marks. This, in turn, helps them punctuate better.

Your child probably won't be able to find all of his errors. You can help, not by pointing out the errors directly, but by reading and putting a mark in the margin on the line of writing which contains an error, as is suggested in the chapter on spelling. You can use an **S** to indicate a spelling error and a **P** to indicate an error in punctuation. Then, see if your child can spot the error. This way, your child has to do the thinking and discover his own mistakes.

After he finds all of the errors, you can help him make corrections with the aid of dictionaries and grammar handbooks. At this point, your child has spent so much time and effort in writing that if there are many errors, you would be kindest to help provide corrections. It is important in all proofreading work to have an attitude of expectancy, which helps to improve upon the work, rather than one of criticism, which finds fault.

When you and your child have corrected all the errors, he can copy the paper over. Then, it is very important that the paper reach its intended audience, either through the mail, on a display, or in a collection. Photocopy your children's best works and send them to interested relatives and friends. Your child can submit exceptionally good pieces for publication. Your child spent a long time to write, edit, proofread, and refine his work. It needs to be valued highly and should not be treated lightly.

Some Final Thoughts on Editing

Stories written by several children provide examples which can be analyzed to summarize the information in these chapters on handwriting, spelling, and mechanics.

Kendrick was asked by his second grade teacher to write a "What if?" story. His creative piece about "opossms" is a delight to read, though it is fraught with spelling and punctuation errors. If his parents focus on these mechanical errors when Kendrick brings home his paper, Kendrick is likely to clip his creative wings. His stories will become shorter and he will use only those words he knows how to spell.

How might Kendrick's parents react to this piece? After reading it, they might say:
"Good job, Kendrick." (Very vague—indefinite praise.)
"Wow, that's a good story!" (A little more specific, but still judgmental.)
"I like the way you thought through how opossums might become extinct." (Much more specific, but still judgmental.)
"I'm glad that opossums have tails, too, and that they are not extinct. Can you tell me more about the fuzzballs?" (They cared to really read what he wrote.)

Because the content is superior to the form of the writing, his parents wouldn't want to comment on the form. For one thing, this is an obvious case of "hurry-up writing"—a first draft done in a twenty-minute writing period.

There is no need for him to revise the piece now unless it is

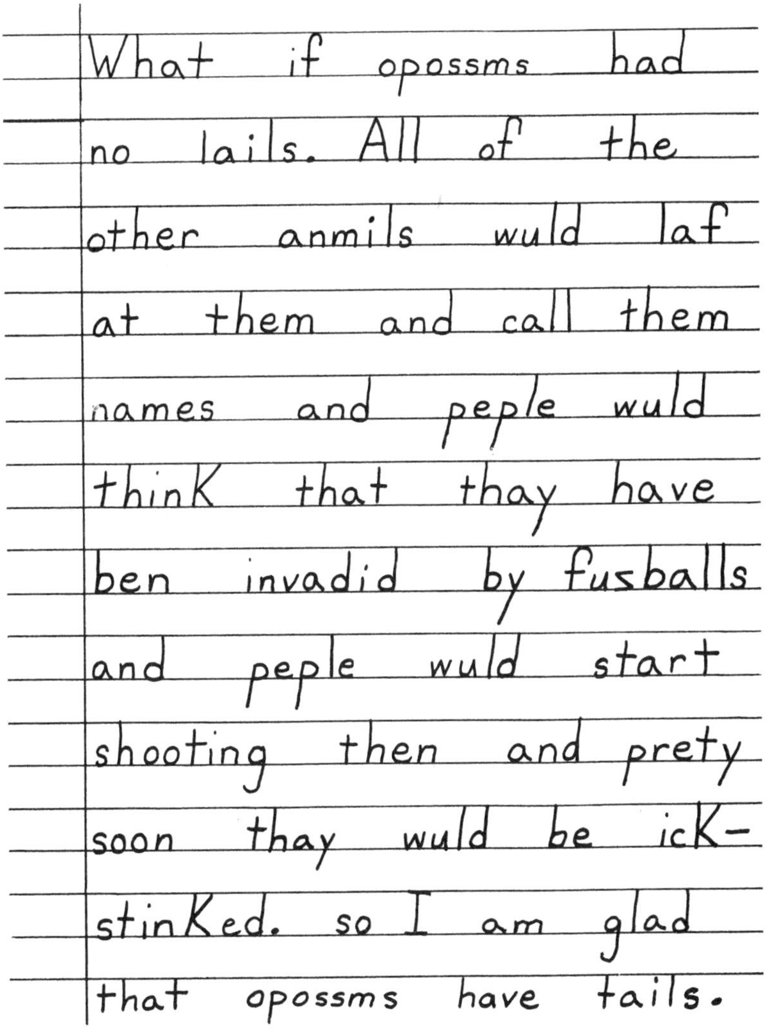

> What if opossms had
> no lails. All of the
> other anmils wuld laf
> at them and call them
> names and peple wuld
> think that thay have
> ben invadid by fusballs
> and peple wuld start
> shooting then and prety
> soon thay wuld be icK-
> stinKed. so I am glad
> that opossms have tails.

Illustration 105

to be sent elsewhere. Parents might take the time to make mental notes about what he is ready to learn, though.

Kendrick's handwriting far surpasses his other technical skills. His letter size, spacing, slant, and letter formation are almost perfect. The uncrossed **t** is an error that proofreading would catch and the reversed **z** will correct itself with time. The uppercase **K** might be taught at a later point when Kendrick is revising a piece he has written at home.

Kendrick has substituted a period for a question mark and omitted several periods. He needs to read this piece out loud to discover where periods are needed. Kendrick's spelling is the weakest of his technical skills. He probably learned how to read by a phonics method so is using primarily phonetical analysis to sound out some words. Kendrick may have an auditory modality strength. He spells a number of common sight words correctly (what, if, had, no, all, of, the, at, them, and, by, from), and displays some visual spelling skill, e.g., tails, opossms, and wuld.

He attempts some hard words and makes them readable (ickstinked for extinct). He needs to look carefully at words to supplement his auditory abilities at spelling. If Kendrick has a spelling box, which words should go in it? Certainly not "extinct," a word he will rarely use again in his writing. Rather, he needs to memorize words like "animals," "would," "people," and "they." He needs the rule for adding **ed** to form the past tense for "invadid."

His parents might not want to deal with any of these educational opportunities in this creative piece. Yet by analyzing it, they can see how their child is developing as a writer. The most important thing is that Kendrick's creative thought be applauded.

This piece is fairly typical of school-assigned writing. He wrote it in thirty minutes and turned it in. Children write much better when they write about what they care about, know about, or have experienced, than when they write on assigned topics. After a visit to Chincoteague Island, Michelle wrote a story of the history of Pony Penning Day in illustration 106.

Michelle's parents kept this story with the family's souvenirs from the trip. They might notice how clear a picture of the ponies' voyage Michelle presents. Michelle uses much more vivid language ("washed off" and "outrider") early in her story than at the end ("went," "made," and "got"). If Michelle wanted to revise her story, she might want to select alternative verbs.

Michelle has not learned yet how to use paragraphs or make transitions in her stories. She might want to write two different stories, one about the history and one about her own experiences.

One a long time ago there was
a Spanish galleon going to Peru
There were ponies to work
in the mines on it. But
~~the~~ a storm was ap-
proaching. It knocked
the ship on her side.
The ponies were wash-
ed off. This happend
near Assateague,
the outrider of little Chincoteauge. The ponies, some-
how w, swam to it. They
began to think of it
as "their home."

But pretty soon more poni&
were born. And more and
more. Soon the island
was overflowing with
ponies. And so, people
from Chincoteauge, came
on their horses and rounded the Spanish ponies up.
They made it a holiday.
"Pony Penning Day." One day
We went to Pony Penning
Day. We camped at Toms
Cove. It was so hot. But
we were lucky. We got
under a bush. We saw the
ponies swim over. We got
pictures.

Illustration 106

The mechanics of the piece are excellent. Michelle writes with voice, as she would talk, underlining for emphasis. Her handwriting might be improved by using lined paper and by writing more slowly, if she were to revise her piece. She needs to learn the "ed rule" for making words past tense and how to use apostrophes for possession.

Often children retell stories when they are asked to write. How might Brian's parents respond to his version of "Jason and the Golden Fleece" (illustration 107)? Actually Brian's piece is the opposite of Kendrick's. His handwriting is legible and his spelling and punctuation are practically flawless, but his story leaves questions in the reader's mind, such as:

- Why (or how) was the king evil?
- Who warned him?
- Why did Jason have to get a Golden Fleece to get the throne?
- What is a Golden Fleece?
- How did Medea, a princess, help Jason?
- Why did Jason rule alone?

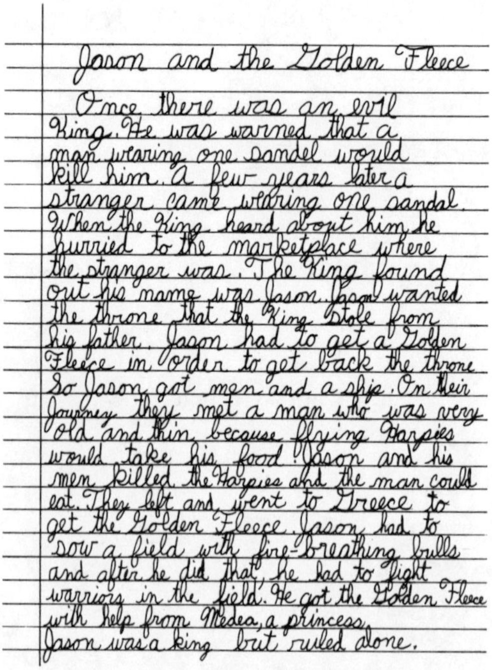

Jason and the Golden Fleece

Once there was an evil King. He was warned that a man wearing one sandel would kill him. A few years later a stranger came wearing one sandel. When the King heard about him, he hurried to the marketplace where the stranger was. The King found out his name was Jason. Jason wanted the throne that the King stole from his father. Jason had to get a Golden Fleece in order to get back the throne. So Jason got men and a ship. On their journey they met a man who was very old and thin because flying Harpies would take his food. Jason and his men killed the Harpies and the man could eat. They left and went to Greece to get the Golden Fleece. Jason had to sow a field with fire-breathing bulls and after he did that he had to fight warriors in the field. He got the Golden Fleece with help from Medea, a princess. Jason was a king but ruled alone.

Illustration 107

Children's literature is a powerful model for writing. In illustration 108 Christy followed the classic folktale model of having a clever victim outwit a predator. What might her parents notice? She wrote very concisely, using folktale terminology, and had a creative idea. She made no spelling errors. Her handwriting is legible, except where it lacks spacing. Next time Christy writes, her parents might want to fold back the paper so she learns to leave margins. She uses all kinds of punctuation effectively. She capitalizes words for emphasis (DON'T!).

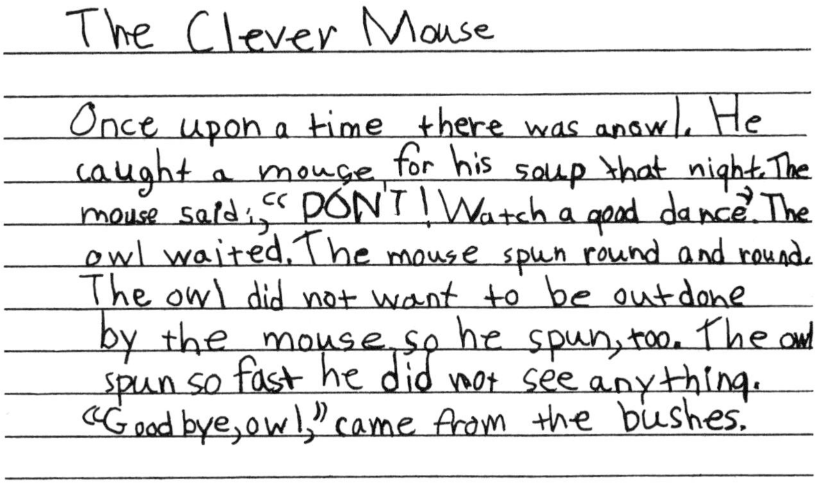

The Clever Mouse

Once upon a time there was an owl. He caught a mouse for his soup that night. The mouse said, "DON'T! Watch a good dance." The owl waited. The mouse spun round and round. The owl did not want to be outdone by the mouse, so he spun, too. The owl spun so fast he did not see anything. "Goodbye, owl," came from the bushes.

Illustration 108

Christy might want to illustrate her tale, or write other tales that follow a similar pattern, then put them into a book of her own folktales.

Chapter 9

Family Writing Experiences

"**D**on't come into my room! I'm not done with my story yet!"
"Mommy, Mommy, I love you. Look in the piano for your first clue!"
"Dear Uncle Simon . . . "

The creative stories that children write in school are often for a teacher who must evaluate children's progress in writing. Although classes sometimes do a unit on letter writing or report writing, rarely does school writing approach the quantity or the variety of writing experiences you can enjoy at home. Some types of writing (personal letters and lists, for example) are far better suited to writing at home than they are to writing at school.

Further, many children feel school experiences are separate from the real world. Reading, spelling, and writing exercises are things done in school, and they bear little relationship to the work and play that take place at home. Home writing experiences, then, serve two primary functions; they show children that writing is a part of the real world—it has a useful function for all adults, even those outside the school environment—and they provide youngsters with a richer variety of writing experiences than they might find in school.

There are different kinds of writing that your children will enjoy with a little encouragement from you. Many of these writing experiences are so minor that you hardly notice them.

Many never occur unless you suggest them; but once they're initiated, they bring hours of enjoyment. Home writing typically falls into three classifications: writing that is mailed or delivered (greeting cards, letters, invitations, or thank you notes); writing that communicates within the family (name cards, diaries, scrapbooks, books, stories, notes, lists, messages, and poems); and writing that is essentially play (signs, labels, tickets, and coupons).

Greeting Cards

Greeting cards are perfect home writing activities. Not only are they fun to make, but they are inexpensive when compared with store-bought cards. Because they are short and repetitive, greeting cards are excellent writing opportunities for very little children just learning to write.

At the same time, greeting cards are excellent writing experiences for mature writers. It takes imagination to condense a message into a short space and provide humor, rhyme, or any other clever writing techniques. Illustration 109 is a rhyme one child made to accompany an Easter card. Cards often combine creative artistry as well as creative text, as in the Valentine in illustration 110. They can be sophisticated writing experiences, requiring many rough drafts and modifications. They are short, so older children don't mind making the necessary revisions to perfect their work.

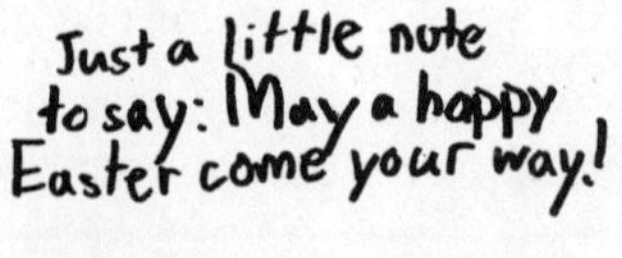

Just a little note to say: May a happy Easter come your way!

Illustration 109

Illustration 110

Greeting cards have another function. In the real world people actually **do** create them. Families often collect examples of homemade cards that have been designed by artist friends. Making greeting cards is not just a writing activity for children, it can be a family activity as well. One family we know makes their Christmas cards every year with each family member contributing. They photocopy the card on colored paper. Children can study published cards and then make their own. They can even send their creations to greeting card companies in the hope that one might be purchased.

Lastly, holidays come at regular intervals so the activity can be repeated and perfected. One-shot writing experiences seldom produce the high quality of writing that repeated experiences might generate. There is a holiday practically once a month, particularly when you include friends' and relatives' birthdays. Homemade cards are often valued more highly than their store-bought equivalents. Of course, children may enjoy decorating and adding to store-bought cards.

Illustration 111 shows one child's purchased Mother's Day card. On the front she wrote, "Love is . . . " Inside, she added "your caring."

Illustration 111

Your child can make greeting cards independently if he has his own supply of stamps, return address stickers, and an address book containing the names of his friends and relatives. He will produce elaborate greeting cards if he has a scrap box containing glitter, ribbon, fabric and paper scraps, wrapping paper scraps, and other decorative materials.

Letter Writing

Letter writing is another activity that is probably better suited to home writing than school writing. The essential concept that letter writing reinforces in young children is that writing communicates. Someone else can read what they write and respond to it, so there is an extrinsic reward for the writer.

In many ways, letter writing is easier than making greeting cards. Older children spend hours on cards, making them complex works of art as well as writing. Personal letters, by their very nature, are personal and do not need to be refined. Personal letters encourage longer writing about personal experiences. They are an excellent preparation for writing stories.

Personal letters have great social value. In today's society, where extended families no longer live together, senior citizens, aunts, uncles, and grandparents are most appreciative audiences for children's letters. Personal letters can provide ties for families who live apart. When children realize how much older relatives appreciate their letters, it makes them feel good about writing.

It is important, though, not to force letter writing. Your child should be able to decide to whom to write. Forcing children to write will result in writing of poor quality and negative feelings about writing. Some families encourage reluctant writers by having a correspondence time each week (a Saturday morning, perhaps) when everyone in the family writes. Other families require each child to write once a week in the winter and once a day in the summer. The topic or type of writing is left to the children and letters often come from these writing sessions. Once children start writing, the letters that they receive provide enough stimulation for them to continue.

You can encourage your child to write to his favorite authors. Authors usually respond to fan mail.

Our daughter wrote to Natalie Savage Carlson. We had just finished reading *A Grandmother for the Orphelines* and Laurel's main question was, "Are you a grandmother?" Mrs. Carlson responded that not only was she a grandmother, she was a great-grandmother, as well! A year later, Laurel wrote to another favorite author, Marguerite Henry, and received the following reply on special stationery with an imprint of Misty on it! Laurel was thrilled, not only with the letter, but with the information it contained.

MISTY

February 1983

Dear Laurel,

What a lovely name! Many a fine poet has been crowned with leaves of laurel.

I'm delighted to know that you like my stories. Yes, the characters are (or were) alive. Some live on in their descendants, like Misty. Stormy is still alive, and she has had seven foals, all but one fillies. Some of them have also had foals, so although Misty died at the age of 26, she has left colts and grandcolts and great grandcolts.

I love your drawings, Laurel, of Misty, The Phantom, the Pied Piper, and Stormy.

Happy reading!

Marguerite Henry

Illustration 112

Children need a place to put the letters they receive. Young children, especially, like to display their letters on bulletin boards, while older children prefer a letter box, letter file, or notebook. A date book stimulates letter and greeting card writing. If children have their own date books with the dates of birthdays and special events marked, they are likely to find reasons for writing letters. Children who keep diaries can remember something to tell other people in letters. One type of writing experience often overlaps another, making children well-rounded writers.

Children who go to camp during the summer enjoy sending and receiving mail. You might include stamped self-addressed postcards in your child's luggage to make writing home easier. You might mail a letter before the child leaves, so he gets mail on the very first day away from home. It is important to keep messages cheerful when writing to children who are away from home.

Traveling presents many opportunities to communicate in writing. Some motels provide stationery and postcards. Post-cards are small, so that writing does not become tedious, yet they are fun to send and to receive. Before starting on a trip you might want to buy some postcard stamps. Sometimes people affix pre-addressed gummed stickers to postcards and save time addressing them as they are traveling. You can make postcards by cutting heavy paper or thin cardboard to postcard size and drawing a picture on one side, leaving the reverse side for the message and address.

Postcards demand concise writing, an important skill to acquire, especially for older children who rarely have exper-iences which cause them to be concise in their writing. Children can learn to omit extraneous information from their postcard messages. So, postcards make ideal writing experiences for both young children and older ones. Your community probably has postcards which your child might enjoy sending to people out of town.

Invitations and Thank You Notes

Invitations and thank you notes are two types of letter writing that warrant special comment. Invitations are short, repetitive writing experiences suitable for young children. At the same time, they are concise enough to stimulate older children who can design them independently. Younger children might prefer to fill in the blanks on store-bought invitations, but older children enjoy the challenge of creating their own invitations. You can ask your child to send out his own invitations to parties, or at least to make invitations along with you, rather than having you do them alone.

Many children incorporate writing invitations into their play. One child put on a performance with her dolls. Her invitation to her parents was sent in an envelope (illustration 113). Children can make programs for their shows and concerts as one child did for a piano concert for her family in illustration 114.

Illustration 113

Two children read the book, *Best-Loved Doll* by Rebecca Caudill (Holt, Rinehart and Winston, 1962), and decided to have a doll party where each child attending brought a favorite doll. They designed invitations from their dolls to the dolls of their friends.

A brother and sister routinely create gymnastics shows on their outdoor play equipment. When their father comes home at night, he usually receives an invitation to a show.

One child invited her parents into her tree house for a

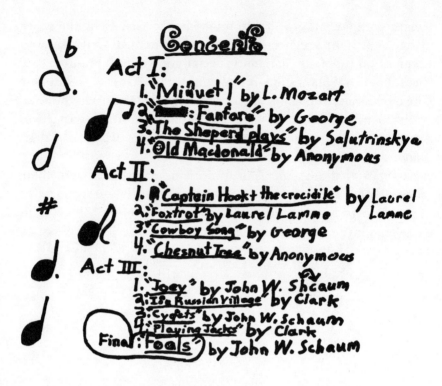

Illustration 114

snack; another invited her parents on a picnic. Children invent lots of reasons to write invitations, especially if you creatively model the idea. One parent invited his daughter to a gymnastics meet by writing her an invitation.

In our neighborhood, the children get together and write invitations to the annual neighborhood Memorial Day Picnic and to a neighborhood cookie party following door-to-door caroling at Christmas. The older children help younger ones write the invitations and deliver them as well. One year, the children got together and, with a parent's help, put on the play "Annie." They sent invitations to the neighborhood to come to the production.

Thank you notes can be drudgery, especially after Christmas or a birthday when children have received a number of gifts from family and friends. Forcing children to write thank you notes can turn them completely away from writing. Some alternatives include letting children make some thank yous by telephone. A distant relative might appreciate a phone call as much as a thank you note. Or, you can spread out writing notes over several weeks. This is especially easy if the opening of presents is spaced. One family lets their children open gifts on the day they arrive in the mail. Gifts are appreciated more one at a time and it is easier to write a thank you note right after receiving the gift than it is several weeks later. Thank you notes can also be kept short and to the point. Often a pretty picture accompanying them is more personal and more enjoyed than the note itself, as in illustration 115.

Illustration 115

Thank you notes may appear less tiresome if they are written at times other than at Christmas and birthdays. Children who are unable to pay for the services of others might say "thank you" to their teachers, dentists, or doctors by drawing a picture for them. You can act as a model yourself by writing notes that say, "Thank you for making your bed this morning without being asked." Children can incorporate thank you notes into their play. In our neighborhood, some retired ladies gave Easter candy to all of the children. The children got together and drew pictures for the ladies as a joint thank you to them. What is important about the thank you note is the message, not the format in which it appears. Creative thinking can make "thank you" an enjoyable thing to say.

Name Cards

Young children are fascinated by people's names, so writing name cards can be a perfect early writing activity. Older children can elaborate on name cards by adding personal touches both in the writing and in the accompanying artwork. In one family, it is the children's responsibility to make place cards for the large family Thanksgiving and Christmas dinners, as in illustration 116. Place cards add a personal and festive touch to dinner parties: one young child enjoyed changing the seating arrangements of the family for every meal by moving place cards around. Another mixed up the letters in each person's name, making finding seats on April Fool's Day a trick.

Illustration 116

Another use for name cards is to label presents at holidays. In one family, these name tags always contain little personal messages. "For my athletic Dad," might contain some running shoes; "For the best mouser in the house," was a catnip mouse for the cat. Again, the homemade tags give gift giving a more personal touch.

Sometimes, at large family gatherings or parties where the guests do not know each other, name tags can help break the ice. One child had invited several children who did not know most of the others to his birthday party. He made name tags for each child and they enjoyed keeping them as party souvenirs.

Signs

Signs are especially appropriate writing activities for young children because they are short, clear messages. They show the power of language to communicate and influence people's behavior.

Adults usually make signs for children before they can write. An adult regularly placed a "wet paint" sign on his children's paintings. One day, Timothy read the sign, recognized a painting as yesterday's painting, and proclaimed that a "dry paint" sign should be made for that painting!

Most early signs are negatives: "Do not touch," "Do not open until Christmas," "Do not come in." One parent put a sign "Please don't ring the bell—nap time," on the doorbell each day when her child went to nap. The sign on the doorbell was part of the pre-nap ritual.

After listening to the song "Sister Suffragette" on her Mary Poppins record, Danielle made a protest sign and marched around the house. The sign said, "Children Have Rights, Too!" She was protesting her parents' decision that there was to be no running inside the house.

Signs can replicate those in the environment—"Stop," "Walk," "Do not pass." They also enhance family communication for children who get tired of being badgered orally to "pick up your clothes" and "brush your teeth thoroughly." They might react more positively to written signs.

Signs and labels become an integral part of play. Several boys made signs to label each part of a play fort they made in a woods. The boys attached their signs to tree branches with tape. Signs and labels quickly transform a clubhouse to a puppet theatre or a playhouse to a spaceship.

Diaries and Scrapbooks

Children write diaries for personal enjoyment. They need no revision. A good time to begin a diary is on a trip. As a going away gift, one family received a cloth-covered notebook in which to make notes about their trip. The gift turned into a scrapbook, for not only did they write in it each night, but they also collected mementos and placed them inside the book. Every evening, each family member wrote a sentence or two about an exciting part of the day that he wanted to remember. Then, they all sat down and read what everyone had written. This album will long be treasured!

Another family received a desk calendar as a gift. Each evening at the supper table, they decided what to record on the calendar about the day's events. Years from now, they will be able to look back at their family's activities for each day of the year. What a marvelous way to record history!

Diaries can be a vent for feelings and frustrations, a completely personal form of writing that nobody else reads. Older children, especially, enjoy writing down their secret feelings about things. How important it is not to violate these personal writings by reading them!

Diaries are written both for the present and for the future, and it is interesting to compare our diaries with those written years ago. Some have been made into books; perhaps the most famous is *The Diary of Ann Frank.* So, we have models to read as we create our own. Each New Year's Eve, one family traditionally reads aloud the diaries of previous years. Then, they write about the most interesting or poignant events of the year that has just ended. Such family traditions can bind families more closely together.

Diaries stimulate other kinds of writing. When a child can't think of something to say in a personal letter, or can't find a topic for a creative writing assignment, he can turn to his diary for some ideas.

You can make a scrapbook after a trip, a holiday, or an exciting family event. Children can also make scrapbooks for their collections (baseball or football cards and clippings, ballet photos and clippings). Over the years, these can become impressive collections with monetary as well as sentimental value.

You can turn photo albums into logs or diaries. One parent labels each photo or page with a brief description of what is going on. Her young daughter learned to read by figuring out these captions of events that she remembered.

One other advantage of diary writing is that it can become habitual. Just as children are encouraged to practice the piano or run daily, they become better writers if they write daily. A diary provides an excellent arena for this systematic type of writing.

Diaries can be logs of observations—science writing done at home. One family records all of the animal tracks they find in the snow surrounding their country home. Another records varieties of birds they see, wild flowers, types of trees, types of cars, and any other topic of interest in their immediate neighborhood. Children can record their observations of plant or animal growth, weather, or other natural phenomena. Precise scientific observation is very different from the narrative chronicling of events in diaries but, in each case, the child is recording something systematically over a period of time. Similarly, homemade calendars with spaces for each day provide children with places to record daily events. After one family used homemade calendars, their daughter made her own calendar of special activities for each day of the week (illustration 117).

Illustration 117

Books and Stories

Children enjoy producing two different types of books. One, like a diary or scrapbook, is a collection of things; the other is a book on one topic. Unlike diaries, which are meant to be read only by the individual who wrote them or by personal friends, books are for more general audiences. Their writing is less personal and therefore more refined.

Recipe books are good examples of expandable collection books. Children enjoy collecting their favorite recipes, especially ones they can cook themselves. Joke books are another example. A book is an excellent place to collect favorite jokes that otherwise would soon be forgotten. One child made a "Funnies Book" by cutting out favorite comic strips from the Sunday paper each week. Small spiral-bound notebooks provide places for these collections.

If children find an ancestor's school book, they will discover that, before basals, children wrote their own school textbooks. I remember finding my mother's science book, complete with illustrations she had drawn herself. She also had a poetry collection that was truly remarkable. If children collect their school work in books and booklets, they can look back over their experiences as writers and observe the changes that have taken place in their own writing.

Homemade books make delightful gifts. When her child was two, one mother began having her son make a book for his father each Christmas. The mother bought a spiral-bound artist's pad and let her son scribble and draw at will. Soon, the child was writing on the pages and the books became a lovely reminder of events in the child's life. Older children write books for younger ones, and ABC books and simple stories with lots of illustrations make fine gifts for preschool children.

Your children will want to make books if you have made books for them. A favorite type of book is one about the children illustrated with photographs of them. They can "read" the book to friends. Books that children write can become part of a family library.

The *Young Author's Program* by Jacque Wuertenberg (Random House, 1982) gives wonderful ideas for both writing and binding homemade books. In this program, children write "what they know about, care about, or have experienced."

Some topics your child might like to explore include:
My Scariest Adventure
What I Remember Most About . . .
I Hope . . .
One Day . . .
What Really Makes Me Happy
My Favorite Poem (or Sport, or Music, etc. and why)
If Only I Could . . .

Aaron drew the Columbia space shuttle before he wrote his story about a blast off (illustration 118 a). It reads, "Once a long, long time ago I was an astronaut and we pushed a button (on) the outside of the ship. It said, '10, 9, 8, 7, 6, 5, 4, 3, 2, 1,

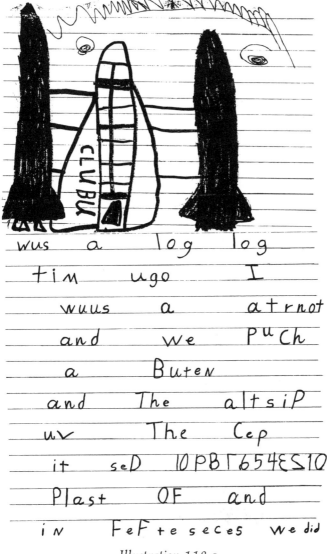

wus a log log
tim ugo I
wuus a atrnot
and we Puch
a Buten
and The altsiP
uv The Cep
it seD 10PBГ654ЕS10
Plast OF and
iN FeF te seCes we did

Illustration 118 a

0—Blast off!' And in fifty seconds we did." Clearly, Aaron had witnessed a lift off, at least on television. Children always write better stories about what they have experienced.

Reginold's fishing story (illustration 118 b) is equally exciting. He wrote, "I was fishing at night for catfish and I hooked an alligator and I reeled it near to me and I yelled, 'Cut the line!' and he swam away and my Grandpa made a string thing to catch the baby alligator. The end."

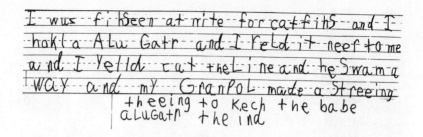

I wus fihseen at nite for catfihS and I hakt a Alu Gatr and I feld it neef to me and I Yelld cut theLine and he Swam away and my GranPoL made a Streeing theeing to Kech the babe aLuGatr the ind

Illustration 118 b

In each case, these boys have fantasized what might have happened in familiar situations. You can collect your child's stories like these in a notebook or scrapbook.

Older children need to write rough drafts of their stories, read them aloud to get feedback, and proofread them before putting their final copies into a book and illustrating them. There are many ways of binding a book. Copy centers can put spiral bindings on homemade books, or you can tie the pages together. A more permanent binding is made by folding pages in half and sewing them together. The end pages can be glued onto a cover that you can make. Find two pieces of cardboard that are larger than your pages and cover them with self-sticking paper or fabric (illustration 119). Having books already bound with blank pages in them encourages book and story writing.

Children can submit their stories to newspapers and magazines for publication. Some publications pay for pieces they publish and some do not. A list of places that publish children's writing is in Appendix C. Some are children's magazines; some are magazines written and edited solely by children; and some are adult magazines and newspapers which publish work by children. Be sure your child understands that not everything he sends in will be accepted for publication but that persistence usually pays off. One family requires its four children to write for fifteen minutes a day during the summer when school is out. They share their writings with each other during the week, and on Friday, revise their best effort and send it out for publication. By the end of the first summer, each child had at least one piece published and, by the end of the second summer, the oldest boy had earned enough to buy himself a

Illustration 119

bicycle—solely from his published writing!

Most children can tell stories way in advance of being able to write. You might then act as a scribe, writing or typing these stories, which your children can later illustrate or refine as they desire. It is fun to file these stories and see how they change over the years. Good storytellers are usually good readers because they know how to anticipate story texts, having created them on their own. Storytelling has almost become a lost art in this country, where people either read or watch television instead of keeping alive the oral storytelling tradition. Aware of how much storytelling builds cohesiveness, some families set aside a time during which they tell stories to each other. One of the functions of storytelling is to pass to future generations tales of their ancestors. If you tape record these stories, they can later be written and kept either in taped or written form for years to come.

Another type of book children write is a report similar to

the ones they write in school. When your children investigate things in their home environments, they can write about them. They might investigate skunks after a pet has been sprayed or they might write about how to grow vegetables in a garden. "How to" books are fun to write. Book writing is closer to school writing than are most other forms of home writing. However, as long as the writing centers upon family interests and activities not being written about in school, it can enjoy a popular place in home writing.

Writing within the Family

Some families write to each other all the time. Parents leave children notes on their pillows or at the breakfast table or tuck a note into lunch boxes. One parent found that during the course of a school year, lunch box notes had served the following functions:

reminders	reading cursive
jokes	giving praise
riddles	suggestions
word games	computer notes
word scrambles	happy thoughts
codes	poems
reading Spanish	song lyrics

It's fun to put variety into lunch box notes. You can buy tiny notecards for special occasions.

Little secret notes provide nice warm feelings when parents are not around. They also serve to vent frustrations. One child vigorously scribbled a "hate note" and handed it to the parent who was the object of those intense feelings. The child could write on paper what he could not express in words about his displeasure. A note is a more powerful form of expression than mere words. After the frustration was vented, the family could laugh the experience off, rather than let it fester and develop into moodiness or become a larger problem.

Parents who write notes to their children find that their notes are reciprocated. One mother found a note in her brown bag lunch! A father found a note in his wallet!

One child who was frustrated because her grandmother's

Illustration 120

dog repeatedly nipped at things wrote the following message to
the dog!

NO NIPPING
And don't nip your ball
With Love From
April to Mike
No Nipping

Children like to write notes to their teachers. One first
grade teacher received many in her mailbox in the classroom.

Dear Mrs. Kolb my mother
tallmeto Stay in

TO: Mrs. Kolb
from: Sara
I Love you
Very much

I Loveyou Mrs. Kolb's

⟨♡⟩

Form Tammy

Mrs. KolB How old are you.
I am 7.   Love Andrea.

Illustration 121

One parent wrote coupons for a child and her friend to redeem after lunch for ice cream cones. Her child responded a few days later with a coupon for some of her chocolate candies. Notes make ordinary affairs, like meals, interesting or special.

Children write notes to the tooth fairy (illustration 122). One child got a note back, and instead of money, a coupon redeemable for an animal miniature for his collection!

Dear tooth fairy, (obiosly Mom ((or dad)) -), 
Please do not take the green chest.
Only take the tooth (which is inside the chest)

Illustration 122

Children enjoy scavenger hunts, when little notes containing clues are placed around the house leading to a special hidden treat. One couple asked two families over for a Christmas party.

During the party each child got to find a treasure, a small gift that was wrapped but hidden somewhere in the house. The children long remembered that party!

In another family, a brother and sister play "Finders Keepers." One hides some money and makes a map for the other to use to find the buried treasure!

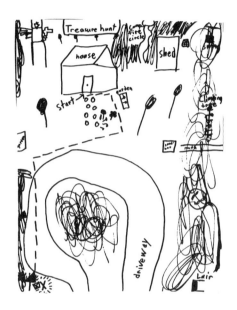

Illustration 123

Sometimes, families write things down to remember them. A calendar posted on the refrigerator is a good place to record family events. The children can copy their activities (school, lessons, allowance days) from one week to another. Parents and children can write notes to remind each other to do things. A chart kept next to a gerbil cage records who fed the gerbils and when. At very early ages, children can be trained to take phone messages and write them down when parents are not available. Family routines are a rich source of these and similar writing experiences.

Making shopping lists is another natural experience for the entire family. Young children automatically make "inventories" as they are learning to write. If they have been writing shopping lists, their inventories are lists of foods. Before a weekly shopping trip, a child can be given a sheet of paper to write out what the parents dictate as they look in their recipe books and refrigerators for their household needs. Spelling doesn't matter, especially if the child comes along on the shopping venture, for the child can read what he wrote. In fact, shopping lists are excellent homemade spelling tests. You can observe the strategies your children use to spell difficult words. Can you figure out the items on the lists in illustration 124?

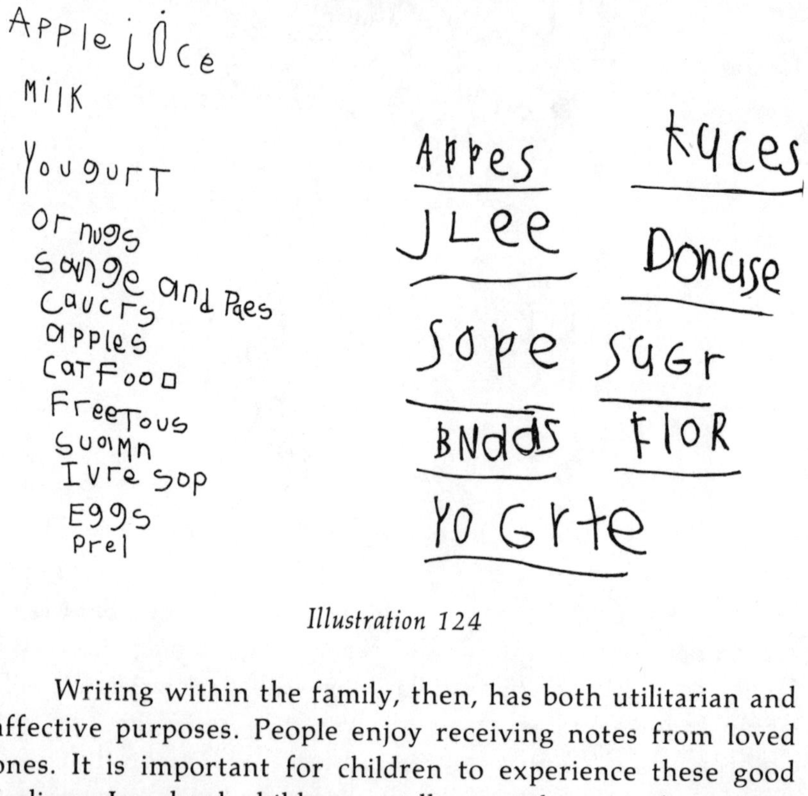

APPle jÛce
MilK
Yougurt
Ornogs
Songe and Paes
Caucrs
apples
CatFooo
FreeTous
Suamn
Ivre Sop
E99s
Prel

Appes   Kuces
JLee   Doncuse
Sope Sugr
BNdds FloR
Yo Grte

Illustration 124

Writing within the family, then, has both utilitarian and affective purposes. People enjoy receiving notes from loved ones. It is important for children to experience these good feelings. In school, children usually write because the teacher tells them to. Functional writing such as making shopping lists, shows children that there are real reasons to write—that writing can make a difference in their lives.

Poetry

Children rarely write poetry except in school. Yet writing poetry can be one of the best ways to share feelings. Young children love rhymes; older children enjoy limericks. If you read

SUMMER

Summer, summer! Summer is here!
Full of warmth full of cheer!
Pretty flowers, many trees,
Hummingbirds, and busy bees!

by Jackie
Fourth Grade

Boats are neat.
Beats are cool.
Boats are big.
Like a swimming pool!

Boats are big.
Boats are small.
Sometimes you find them,
In a shopping mall!

Boats are huge.
Boats are gigantic.
Some boats can even,
Cross the Atlantic.

by Marco Musumeci
Fourth Grade

Staring at the Sky

I'm just lying here, staring at the sky. Watching the birds
and the clouds fly by. Just the grass and I, Staring at the
sky.

by Kip Wilson
Fourth Grade

Illustration 125

poetry and have poetry books around the house, your children appreciate poetry and naturally want to write some. Children who sing a lot of songs enjoy making up new lyrics to melodies they know.

Easy ways to write poetry are to make greeting cards with short rhymes on them or to adjust the words to a familiar tune. "Mary wore her red dress, red dress, red dress," can easily be changed to "Peter wore his blue shoes, blue shoes, blue shoes," and still fit the tune.

Another way to encourage poetry is to appreciate poetic language. One family has a "secret word club." Family members collect secret words that sound good or that sound like the things they represent in meaning. The study of product and business labels can be fascinating. Studying advertising techniques and gimmicks and learning advertising rhymes and jingles make language study fun and develop within children a "word awareness" which is a tremendous asset for a writer.

Not all poetry must rhyme. In his book, *Wishes, Lies and Dreams,* (Random House, 1970) Kenneth Koch tells how he teaches children to write non-rhyming poetry. He asks children to list things, such as "I wish . . . " With minor reworking, these wish lists take on a poetic format. Children learn to work with images (as white as the snow; as smooth as silk) and other word phrases using common ones as examples.

Literature is a potent model for writing poetry. Shel Silverstein is a popular poet. His poems about everyday things and feelings provide interesting models. Periodically, the National Council of Teachers of English gives an award to a children's poet for his life's work in writing poetry. Those who have won this award so far include David McCord, Aileen Fisher, Myra Cohn Livingston, Eve Merriam, and Karla Kuskin. Another popular poet and compiler of poetry is Lee Bennett Hopkins. Old time poets like Robert Louis Stevenson and A.A. Milne continue to be popular with children. You can find poets whose work you particularly enjoy and then share the poems with your family. After sharing poetry, it becomes natural for children to write their own.

Writing during Play

Children incorporate writing into their play. You can encourage this by being sure that paper and markers are available. Most children at one time or another have a pretend store with items for sale. If you provide press-on labels, children can price each item for sale. Since writing numbers is harder than writing alphabet letters (because it is done less frequently), this is an especially good writing experience. You might provide older children with old blank checks to pay for items. Children make out coupons and have sales, all of which provide writing as well as mathematical experiences.

In our neighborhood, the children are always selling something. For garage sales, they set up lemonade stands, which require advertising and sign-making. Garage sales themselves give children an opportunity to sell old toys and games, labeling each one with prices. Two enterprising young girls went around the neighborhood selling roly polys (worm-like crustaceans plentiful in sandy Florida soils). When they found that most adults were in no need of roly polys, they made a sign which read: "Roly polys for sale. Big ones—2 cents, little ones—1 cent. We babysit them free!" Soon they had many takers.

Children make and exchange tickets during play. They

might make tickets for a puppet show and distribute them to family members who provide an eager audience. Two girls wrote invitations to a puppet show, gave out pretend tickets, labeled child-size seats with seat numbers, and provided their viewers with a program—four writing activities for one performance!

Children might give each other tickets to ride on their bicycles or they might write out tickets when playing police officer. They make airline tickets and railroad tickets for dolls who pretend to take rides. A ticket punch guarantees that transportation tickets will be made.

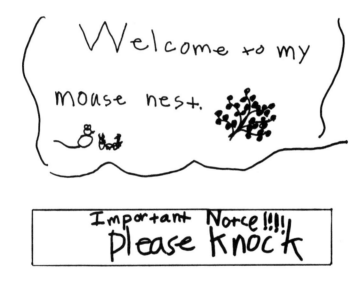

Illustration 126

Writing can become an integral part of play. Illustration 126 is a welcome sign found on the door of Venus's room. Two boys made a "Do Not Disturb" sign for a home they built for their worms. They made "wet paint" signs to guard their paintings. They labeled their constructions of interlocking blocks. A group of youngsters made a float at homecoming time and labeled the side of it, "The Balloon Bunch." Some other children made a pretend ice cream truck and labeled the flavors they were selling. Children make license plates for their bikes and signs for their clubhouses, forts, treehouses, and other special places. When they play restaurant, they create menus. Little pads provide places for little secretaries to write notes. Some children held a doll show and made prizes for each doll participant. Then they made awards for members of their families (illustration 127). Labeling and making signs can be encouraged as a part of play by parents who are sensitive to children's desires to express themselves in writing. Many of these play ideas come from the children themselves; others, you can suggest. If you supply the props, play writing is more likely to occur.

Illustration 127

Obviously, no one family could or would want to use all of the suggested activities mentioned in this chapter. Writing activities within the home can be overdone. Forced writing is worse than no writing at all. But as long as these home writing activities appear to have merit in your individual family situation, they can foster an environment that encourages children to enjoy writing. If you have been neglecting this aspect of your home environment you might consider moving toward giving writing a more central role in your daily routines.

Chapter 10

Some Related Considerations

Writing is important. If children grow up writing and reading, they grow up thinking about language in a unique way. Writing makes different demands upon thought than speaking does. Writing is planned and can be revised. Created with premeditation, it is a more permanent statement than talk. The very qualities that differentiate the written word from the spoken word make writing more emphatic.

Writers are readers, for everything that is written is read, usually several times. Children carry their writings around, saying, "Won't you read what I wrote?" Or, "Don't read this yet, it is a secret message." As they write, many children read and reread what they have written.

Josh was encouraged by his first grade teacher to keep a log or journal of his activities throughout the summer as he had done in his first grade classroom. His mother insisted that he write just a sentence or two in his journal every day. When I saw Josh in August, he proudly showed me two spiral-bound notebooks that were filled with his writings. He simply loved to go back and read over all the entries he had made for each day of the summer. His mother reported that prior to this, Josh seldom chose to read books that were as long as his diary. It wasn't until he had written and then read his long diary that he learned to enjoy reading longer storybooks!

Writing is quite an accomplishment for children. In some ways, it resembles learning to play a musical instrument or learning how to play a sport. As one progresses, one can look back and feel a sense of accomplishment derived from hard work. Writing gives children a sense of power. Imagine being able to control adults by saying, "You are to come to my cave when I ring the triangle," or "Stop and pay toll before entering." Writing gives children a sense of fulfillment when the piece of writing they have worked hard on communicates.

In addition to all of the educational values of learning to write, children find that writing is fun. In one classroom where children were read to frequently and given lots of opportunities to write, the teacher lamented that the children were ignoring all of the toys. They were so eager to become literate that they spent every free moment either reading, writing, or drawing. These children had learned early in life that reading and writing are satisfying leisure time activities.

Oral Language Development and Writing

Children's writing, especially in the beginning stages, is highly dependent upon their oral language ability. Word play greatly enhances children's oral and written language. In a similar fashion, the way children tell stories sets the stage for the way they will write stories when their motor development is such that they can sustain long periods of handwriting.

Children's storytelling abilities develop from their abilities to comprehend stories they have heard in literature. Children like to hear some stories over and over again. As they are listening, they are developing a story schema, or mental picture, about how a story is formed. For example, stories have a formal opening. In most fairy tales, it is the familiar, "Once upon a time." Stories have a plot with a sequence to it, characters that are described, and a formal closing.

Because of their highly predictable format, characters that are either totally good or evil, and repetitious sequence of events, fairy tales are especially good for helping children acquire comprehension skills and storytelling ability. Usually, comprehension develops as children learn to retell a familiar story. Children might retell the story first using the pictures in a book, then using a flannel board with puppets, or they might dramatize the story. Next, they will orally tell the story without any props. Finally, children will take the story pattern and create an original story.

Until children can write, you need to write their stories for them acting as a secretary. At first your child will not pace the dictation and you will have to make it clear that he must go slowly enough for you to write the words. When children realize that the words they are speaking are the same words that are appearing on paper, they adjust their speed of storytelling to match the pace of the secretary. If children in their initial years as writers are not given the opportunity to tell their stories so an adult can write them down, they will perceive of writing as little more than handwriting. Their ability to tell stories (and therefore to write them) atrophies from lack of use. It is important, then, for children to be able to dictate their long stories while they are independently writing less lengthy texts.

As they acquire the formal story elements of opening, plot, characterization, and closing, children's stories grow to sound more like the stories in literature. They improve in other ways as well; they develop cohesion. One sentence is linked to the next with referents that match previous words. For example, an early story might have the three bears leaving their porridge to cool, followed by, "Then he took a walk in the woods." The word "he" might refer to any one of the three bears, and therefore is unclear. In a more mature telling of the same story, the three bears would always be referred to as "they." The links from one sentence or paragraph to the next would always be clear.

The vocabulary used in the stories shows a progression from very general nouns and verbs to very specific ones. Instead of leaving their cereal, the bears, in a more mature text, leave their porridge. Instead of "going for a walk," the bears "amble through the woods."

The stories children tell show the same kind of development as their written stories. Because they are longer and are dictated to an adult, oral storytelling helps children understand the goal of their writing development. They see that, even though they can't yet write long stories on their own, in the not-too-distant future their writing will be more complex and lengthy.

Especially for Fathers

Although virtually any idea in this book is appropriate for

mothers and fathers, there are a few pointers which might form a special message to fathers. Children who are fortunate enough to have two parents benefit in different ways from interaction with each one. This generalization applies to writing as well. For example, in one family, when the mother wrote little notes for the children's lunch boxes, they were sentences, such as: "I'm eager to see your soccer game." The father's messages were usually poems: "See you at two; I love you," or, "My pick for the soccer kick is YOU!" Needless to say, the children appreciated both messages.

It is important not to leave writing to one parent. Parents who are divorced find that writing helps strengthen the ties between the absent parent and the children. Writing has a utilitarian function as well. It informs the absent parent of what has been going on in the child's life. You can send children visiting a parent (or any relative) reminders in writing about things they need to do. Some children collect the letters they receive from a parent or special friend and read them over and over at a later time.

Similarly, if you travel, you can communicate in writing with your children. You can send postcards, letters, and notes through the mail. One father left a series of notes to be placed in his child's lunch box on the days he was gone. Little reminders assure children that even though we are not present, we still love them and support them.

Parents who appreciate their children's drawings and writings display them not only on the walls of their homes but also at their work places. Many fathers frame and hang their children's work in their offices. Cherishing pieces that were carefully created as gifts draws family members closer together.

Stories, poems, labeled pictures, or other creations make wonderful gifts. One father has his children create one especially nice written piece as a Mother's Day gift each year. Writings about "Mom" will be treasured for years to come. And of course, moms could try the reverse for Father's Day! One father made a collage of the sayings his children created for Mother's Day. It made the little children feel important to see their work combined with that of their older siblings.

Fathers do have a special role in helping their children grow up writing. Because they tend to be absent from their children for longer periods of time than some mothers are, there is more opportunity to send notes and messages back and forth with their children. If fathers are home as much as moms are, the benefits of having both parents involved in writing with children are great. Inevitably, each parent has something unique to bring to the writing realationship.

Especially for Grandparents

Grandparents can have a powerful impact upon children's writing development, especially if they live far from their grandchildren. They are even better informal teachers than parents because they are far less critical.

If grandparents live at a distance, the most inspiring contribution they can make is to establish regular written communication with their grandchildren. Instead of writing one letter to several children in a household, it is helpful if they write a separate communication to each child, individualizing the message, if possible. Grandparents can, in this way, help their grandchildren establish a regular writing habit. When I found in my parents' attic all of the letters that my grandmother had sent to me over the years, I could readily see why I loved my grandmother so much. In her letters she always inquired about my home and school activities. She took an avid interest in what I was doing and she lavishly praised all of my accomplishments. With an audience as receptive as that, no wonder I loved to write personal letters! I am sure that my grandmother was far less critical than my parents because they saw my activities from a much closer perspective and were more apt to reprimand me for the negative things that I did (which Grandmother probably never even knew about).

Grandmother did something else which made her letters at holiday time special. She enclosed a little money or trinket of some sort in the envelope with a holiday greeting card. My grandmother was not wealthy, but she always saw to it that I had a greeting card and some little item for a celebration. I still have several hankies she sent me along with other mementos— little dolls, boxes, and foreign coins. Naturally, whenever grandparents send their grandchildren something in the mail, children want to write back to thank them.

Grandparents serve another function in family writing activities. They help to preserve the family heritage by recording events of the past for their families. These recordings can be tape recordings which other family members can transcribe, or they can be in the form of diaries or a series of letters. Parents can encourage grandparents to tell about the "olden days" from time to time so that these early family memoirs can be written down or recorded and preserved. Grandparents are our best sources of oral and written histories. They help children develop skill at notetaking and writing historical accounts, which might even lead to the writing of historical fiction.

Even if grandparents live right around the corner, they can still communicate with their grandchildren in writing. When you go away on vacation, Granny makes a perfect friend to whom a postcard might be sent. Sometimes, grandparents whose lifestyles are more formal than ours enjoy having children make place cards for the dining table. None of these interactions is directly for the purpose of teaching. They are just realistic, wonderful opportunities for grandparents and grandchildren to become closer through writing.

Another function grandparents serve is that of audience for the writings of their grandchildren. Your children can send photocopies of their best stories to their grandparents. Children's writings also make excellent presents to receptive grandparents at holiday times.

In a society where extended families are rare, family ties are strengthened through communication. Grandparents can help maintain close ties with all family members by serving as the center of this communication system.

Leave It to the Schools?

Many parents claim that things such as reading and writing should be left to the schools; parental help may confuse children, they believe. Or, some parents may feel unqualified to "teach" writing.

Some schools rarely have children write. When standardized test scores decline, teaching is directed at helping children achieve better scores. Therefore, there is more emphasis on teaching skills and less practice in reading and writing for communication. If you don't encourage writing and provide a time and place for writing to occur, your children may go through school writing only a few pieces a year.

Even when schools do teach and encourage writing, children's values and life habits are still formulated at home. Children may learn how to read and write in school, but they won't be avid readers and writers unless the home environment encourages those activities.

You not only need to encourage writing at home, but also you should exert whatever influence you have to place meaningful composing experiences into the school curriculum. Several school curricula have children write compositions on a daily basis. You might want to get information from any of these programs to share with your local public school:

Director of Language
  Arts Instruction
Grosse Pointe Michigan
  Public School System
389 St. Clair Avenue
Grosse Pointe, MI 48230

Director of Language
  Arts Instruction
Weehauken Public Schools
Weehauken, NJ 07087

Atkinson, New Hampshire Public Schools
c/o Dr. Donald Graves
The Writing Process Laboratory
University of New Hampshire
Durham, NH 03824

How Children Describe Writing

It seems appropriate to end this book with some children's views on writing. If their comments don't convince you that writing is valuable and important, no amount of adult persuasion will.

"I like writing, especially notes to my friends because it makes them feel good."

"You know what I want to learn to do more than anything else in the world? I want to learn how to write!"

"Writing? Well it's important, 'cause how're you gonna remember things if you don't write them down?"

"No, I can't read, but I can write!"

"Did I get any mail today? I did? Oh boy, a letter from Kelly!"

"Mommy, Mommy, come here! This story in my head's just got to come out!"

"I'm going to be an author when I grow up."

Growing Up Writing

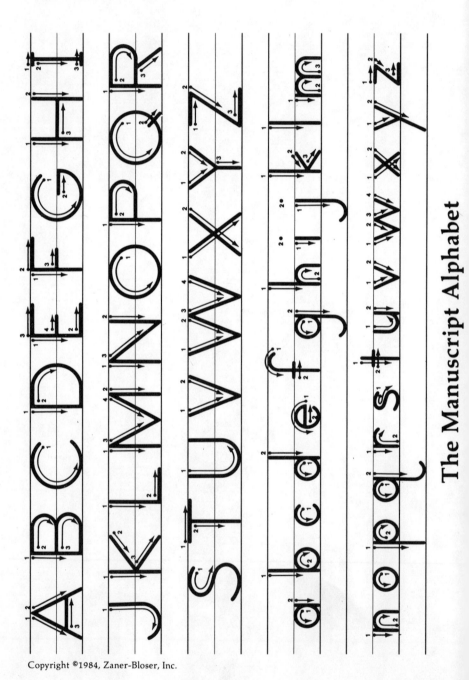

The Manuscript Alphabet

The Cursive Alphabet

Periodicals That Publish Children's Writing

Chickadee

The Young Naturalist Foundation
59 Front Street E
Toronto, Ontario M5E 1B3
CANADA
Age range: 4-8. The Environment.
First Issue: 1979. Thirty-two
pages. Ten issues a year.
Accepts expository letters for
"Something To Chirp About," a
monthly feature.

Children's Digest

P.O. Box 567B
Indianapolis, IN 46206
Age range: 8-10. Health, Safety,
and Nutrition. First Issue: 1950.
Forty-eight pages. Eight issues a
year. Accepts poetry, jokes,
riddles, stories up to 700 words.
In "What Do You Think?" children write about questions asked
in an earlier issue.

Child Life

P.O. Box 567B
Indianapolis, IN 46206
Age range: 7-9. Health, Safety,
and Nutrition. First issue: 1921.
Forty-eight pages. Eight issues a
year. Accepts poetry, stories up
to 500 words, jokes, and riddles.

"All Yours" features letters to the
editor.

Children's Playmate

P.O. BOX 567B
Indianapolis, IN 46206
Age range: 5-7. First Issue: 1929.
Forty-eight pages. Eight issues a
year. Accepts artwork and poetry.

Cobblestone

20 Grove Street
Peterborough, NH 03458
Age range: 8-14. History. First
Issue: 1979. Forty-eight pages.
Twelve issues a year. Accepts
"Letters to Ebenezer," both ex-
pository and personal narrative.

Cricket

P.O. Box 100
LaSalle, Il 61301
Age range: 6-12. Literary. First
issue: 1973. Sixty-four pages.
Twelve issues a year. Accepts
children's contributions for "Let-
terbox" and "Cricket League."
Cricket League contests are held
monthly in two of three categories—
drawing, poetry, and short story.
Rules for the contests are
explained in each issue.

Ebony Jr!
820 S. Michigan Avenue
Chicago, IL 60605
Children. First issue: 1973.
Forty-eight pages. Ten issues a
year. Accepts original poems,
short stories, essays, jokes,
riddles, cartoons, and artwork.

The Electric Company
200 Watt Street
P.O. BOX 2924
Boulder, CO 80322
Age range: 6-9 General Interest.
First Issue: 1974. Thirty-six pages.
Ten issues a year. Unsolicited
material accepted, including jokes
for "Tickle Yourself." Specific
guidelines for other contributions
such as poetry, short stories, and
essays appear in each issue.

**Faces, The Magazine about
People**
20 Grove Street
Peterborough, NH 03458
Age range: 8-10. History. Pub-
lished in cooperation with the
American Museum of Natural
History in New York City. First
Issue: 1984. Thirty-six pages. Ten
issues a year. Accepts letters to
the editor, both expository and
personal narrative.

Highlights for Children
803 Church Street
Honesdale, PA 18431
Age range: 2-12. General Interest.
First Issue: 1946. Forty-two pages.
Eleven issues a year. Accepts
original poetry, short stories,
unfinished stories, jokes, riddles,
brief personal narratives, letters
to the editor, and "Creatures

Nobody Has Ever Seen." All
contributions acknowledged.

Humpty Dumpty
P.O. Box 567B
Indianapolis, IN 46206
Age range: 4-6. Health, Safety,
and Nutrition. First Issue: 1952.
Forty-eight pages. Eight issues a
year. Accepts children's artwork.

Jack and Jill
P.O. Box 567B
Indianapolis, IN 46206
Age range: 6-8. Health, Safety,
and Nutrition. First Issue: 1938.
Forty-eight pages. Eight issues a
year. Accepts artwork, poetry,
jokes and riddles, letters to the
editor, and short stories up to 500
words.

Jam
#202 56 The Esplanade
Toronto, Ontario M5E 1A7
CANADA
Age range: 10-16. General Inter-
est. First Issue 1980. Forty pages.
Six issues a year. Accepts poetry.
publishes children's work on a
semi-regular basis.

National Geographic World
17th and M Streets N.W.
Washington, DC 20036
Age range: 8-13. General Interest.
First Issue: 1975. Thirty-two to
forty pages. Twelve issues a year.
Accepts children's letters for
monthly "Mailbag" column.
Special submissions are occasionally requested. Guidelines for
these appear in each issue.
Children's poetry and fiction are
not published.

Odyssey
P.O. Box 92788
Milwaukee, WI 53202
Age Range: 8-14. Astronomy and Space Science. First Issue: 1979. Forty pages. Twelve issues a year. Accepts artwork, stories, and essays—usually based on suggested topics. Regular columns include "Letters to the Editor," "Future Forum," and essays dealing with various topics. Special contests such as a cover contest are held periodically. Science Fair projects are often featured. Guidelines appear in monthly issues.

Owl
The Young Naturalist Foundation
59 Front Street East
Toronto, Ontario M5E 1B3
CANADA
Age range: 8-14. The Environment. First issue: 1976. Thirty-two pages. Ten issues a year. Accepts material for "All Your Own," a contest feature. Contests range from writing topics to photography. General guidelines available in each issue.

Penny Power
256 Washington Street
Mt. Vernon, NY 10053
Age range: 8-14. Consumer Education. First issue: 1980. Twenty-two pages. Six issues a year. Accepts letters to the editor. "Pen Power" encourages children to share their ideas and suggestions. Often, specific topics are introduced on this page and children are encouraged to write in response to a given topic.

Turtle
P.O. Box 567B
IndianapoliS, IN 46206
Age range: 2-5. Preschool Health. First Issue: 1979. Forty-eight pages. Eight issues a year. Accepts children's artwork.

NEWSPAPER SUPPLEMENTS

"The Children's Page"
The Christian Science Monitor
One Norway Street
Boston, MA 02115
Age range: 5-18. General Interest. Weekly feature available through subscription to **The Christian Science Monitor.** Accepts poems, sketches, computergraphics, B/W photos, short stories, essays (150 word limit). Send contributions to the attention of The Children's Page Editor.

Pennywhistle Press
Box 500-P
Washington, DC 20044
Age range: 4-12. General Interest. Weekly feature available through purchase of subscribing newspaper. Accepts drawings, jokes, riddles, and letters to "Mailbag." Contests are also held periodically.

MAGAZINES BY CHILDREN

The McGuffey Writer
400 A McGuffey Hall
Miami University
Oxford, OH 45056
Age range: preschool-18. Children's Writing. First Issue: 1978. Twelve Pages. Three issues a year. Accepts poetry, cartoons,

and artwork as well as short stories and essays. (Word limit is two typewritten pages.) Longer works are often excerpted.

Stone Soup
Children's Art Foundation
P.O. Box 83
Santa Cruz, CA 95063
Age range: 6-13. Literary. First Issue: 1973. Forty-eight pages. Five issues a year. Accepts poetry, short stories, drawings, and book reviews. Longer works which describe personal experiences, are encouraged. Children interested in doing book reviews should address their correspondence to Jerry Mandel. **Stone Soup** will provide the book to be reviewed.

Also available is **Stone Soup in the Classroom,** a guide intended for teachers.

Wombat
Journal of Young People's Writing and Art
365 Ashton Drive
Athens, GA 30606
Age range: 6-18. Young People's Creative Work in Art and Writing. First Issue: 1979. Thirty-two pages. Four issues a year. Accepts original poetry, short stories (shorter stories preferred), prose, essays, artwork (B/W preferred or color with strong line definition), cartoons, puzzles, and book reviews.

It is advisable to find the publication in a library or write for a copy before submitting work because many publications have very specific criteria for how the work must be submitted. Most will send you information in addition to what is found in the publication.

Index

About the Author

Linda Leonard Lamme is Professor of Elementary and Early Childhood Education at the University of Florida. She received her Ph.D. from Syracuse University. Dr. Lamme is the senior author of *Raising Readers* (Walker & Co., 1980) and *Learning to Love Literature* (National Council of Teachers of English, 1981). She is an active member of the International Reading Association, the National Association for the Education of Young Children, and the National Council of Teachers of English. Dr. Lamme, her daughter, and her husband enjoy writing as a family.